We can juggle being a mum,
a wife, a friend and a career.

We laugh when inside we feel
like everything is falling apart.

We are there when we need to be,
even if it means staying up all night.

We adjust and adapt to whatever life
seems to throw at us.

We believe in the impossible
even when logic tells us not to.

We are the teller of stories
and memory keepers.

We are the secret keeper and
dream maker.

We are women. We can take on
almost any storm life may throw our way.

ANON

THE JUGGLE

INSPIRATIONAL STORIES FROM MUMS JUGGLING IT ALL

STEPH ADAMS & SAMANTHA BRETT

FOR ME, BEING MUM-IN-CHIEF IS AND ALWAYS WILL BE JOB NUMBER ONE.

MICHELLE OBAMA

HAVING KIDS—THE RESPONSIBILITY OF REARING GOOD, KIND, ETHICAL, RESPONSIBLE HUMAN BEINGS—IS THE BIGGEST JOB ANYONE CAN EMBARK ON.

MARIA SHRIVER

AS A MOTHER I ALWAYS HAVE SOMETHING BETTER TO BE DOING. I LOVE WORK BUT I'M LESS TOLERANT OF MY TIME BEING WASTED.

CINDY CRAWFORD

Photo credit: Chantell Bianchi

This book is dedicated to all the mums on the planet for your tireless dedication, endless love, boundless energy and wonderful contribution to your bundles of joy and, in turn, to the world in helping guide the next generation. We honour you and we salute you. Thank you for everything you do.

To my daughter Harper, thank you for introducing me to The Juggle and making me a better person and mother with your infectious smile and beautiful personality. You are sunshine.
Samantha Brett

To my dear boys, Bailey, Joshua and Joel. Thank you for all the love you give me every day. Even through the chaos, the ups and the downs, we continue to laugh! Never a dull moment!
Steph Adams

MOTHERHOOD: POWERED BY LOVE, FUELLED BY COFFEE, SUSTAINED BY WINE.

The Juggle

Noun:

(n) The art of balancing family, work, life and kids, often without recognition, thanks, acknowledgement or sleep.

CONTENTS

THE JUGGLE

Photo credit: Mark Stanley

INTRODUCTION

Wise women will tell you that having a baby doesn't mean you can't still do it all, just not all at the same time. But that doesn't stop many mothers from trying to tackle everything head-on all at the same time, including your intrepid authors, and often finding ourselves failing miserably.

Take the day of the book launch for our first collaborative book together, *The Game Changers*. That morning, Samantha was woken up at 3 a.m. by her baby having a meltdown. Steph's toddler decided that midnight was the time for playing with Mummy and Daddy while her newborn was woken up by the commotion and refused to go back to sleep. By 9 a.m. we both arrived flustered with moments to spare before the launch of our book, which was an intimate brunch hosted by Julie Bishop, then Australia's Minister for Foreign Affairs. Samantha's dress split just before she left the house. Steph's feet were still swollen from giving birth. We were hungry, tired and a mess.

When we stood up to say our speeches and had nothing prepared other than some scribblings on a food-stained scrap of paper, the other mums in the room nodded in silent recognition. They knew what it took to simply get out of the house some days, let alone stand up in front of a crowd and give a speech! With make-up on! And photographers! And the press! And the Foreign Minister!

The Game Changers, written while Sam was heavily pregnant and Steph was navigating the sticky, sleep-deprived waters of being a new mum – much to our surprise and indeed the world – featured one of the only interviews with Meghan Markle, conducted only a few months before the news broke that she was dating Prince Harry.

Under the impression that she was a little-known actress who was blazing her own unique trail, speaking out about important causes and using her own voice to share her personal opinions for her blog, we thought she was a rare breed of actress and that she'd be an ideal candidate to sit alongside our Game Changers like Arianna Huffington and Laurie Adams, who we'd already secured for the book.

A few months after the book was launched, we were booked for a live interview with a television station in the UK to talk about our experience with Meghan, now the most famous woman in the world. That meant driving to the television station affiliate building in Sydney during the afternoon peak-hour traffic in order to make it in time for London's morning news. With babies bathed, nappies changed, bottles filled, babysitters hired, make-up slapped on and power-suit jackets at the ready, we jumped in the car and began the long drive.

With minutes to spare we arrived at the studios, only to be told by the car park attendant that we were in fact at the wrong building, and the one we were supposed to be at was another hour away. With no petrol, no mobile phone battery and no idea where we were going, we jumped back in the car and prayed that our hatchback wouldn't break down in the middle of the highway as we weaved in and out of crawling traffic.

Huffing and puffing, mascara smudged and hair frizzed, we arrived at the studio a little worse for wear. Sam noticed she was missing an earring, Steph had a food stain down the front of her shirt and in all the commotion we had forgotten to actually prepare what we were saying. #Mumlife. Of course we wouldn't have it any other way.

It's no surprise that 43 per cent of highly qualified women with children are leaving their careers due to the difficulties of The Juggle. In fact, throughout our research for this book, many working mums confessed to us that they are riddled with guilt when they leave home and their bub to head to the office (even though sometimes it's a relief to get there in one piece!). But what surprised us the most is that mums who've chosen to stay at home to raise their families sometimes share similar feelings. Guilt is replaced with shame, embarrassment or even regret as a result of societal pressures and expectations surrounding the fact that they've left their important jobs and successful careers they've worked so hard for to spend life at home.

In our mothers' and grandmothers' eras, quitting their jobs to raise a family was done without a second thought. Nowadays we're often encouraged, sometimes even expected, to jump back into the workforce with the same passion and dedication that we once had. Which becomes impossible when you're trying to juggle it all. And as so many know all too well, something eventually has to give.

Even new mum and tennis champion Serena Williams has admitted returning to work after giving birth was a major struggle, especially when she missed her daughter's big milestone. 'She took her first steps,' she tweeted. 'I was training and I missed it. I cried.' She dedicated her incredible Wimbledon run to all the mums out there, struggling, juggling and simply powering on because, well, there is no other choice. 'Some days, I cry. I'm really sad. I've had meltdowns. It's been a really tough eleven months. If I can do it, you guys can do it too.'

As you'll read in these pages, every mum we've interviewed – no matter their age, background, career or relationship status – shares the same challenges, juggles and struggles. We're all simply trying to do our best with what we've got, and to arm our little cherubs with enough strength, wisdom, strong values and sense of self as we can, without beating ourselves up too much over the tough days (which often turn into the most hilarious mum moments!).

The idea for *The Juggle* stemmed from that day when we were so close to missing an international promotional interview for our bestselling book, yet hours earlier we knew that our little cherubs were the only things that mattered in the world and that everyone else would to have wait. They did wait, but we certainly emerged from that experience with the realisation that women can't actually do it all at the same time, nor should we be expected to, but we can certainly give it a red-hot go. And always carry a spare mobile phone charger!

Samantha Brett & Steph Adams

MEGHAN MARKLE
MOTTO

€1.14 0.23%
CASTLE HILL, WINDSOR
LIVE
SYDNEY
ROYAL WEDDING
FINAL PREPARATIONS ARE UNDER WAY FOR PRINCE HARRY
AND MEGHAN MARKLE'S WEDDING IN WINDSOR TOMORROW

THE DAILY EDITION

TALKING lifestyle RADIO
TALKING lifestyle

JUGGLING IT ALL

1. Instil confidence

2. Make a calendar

3. Prioritise

4. Eliminate guilt

5. Go with the flow

6. Find your army

7. Eliminate comparisons

8. Create 'me' time

9. Take time to find the joy

SHANISTY IRELAND

WHEN YOU BECOME A MUM, THE LAST THING YOU WANT TO DO IS FEEL JUDGED, BECAUSE EVERYONE IS TRYING TO DO THE BEST THEY CAN.

JESSICA ALBA

Photographer Sam Elsom | Creative by Sheree Commerford of Captain And the Gypsy Kid

TERESA PALMER

ACTRESS, WRITER, MUM

'I will always remember how magical childhood felt: colourful, full of excitement and completely enchanting.'

My childhood was spent running around in the beautiful Adelaide Hills, climbing trees, rollerblading, horseriding, building forts and playing hide and seek in the dark with my mum and my friends. At my best friend Kat's house we'd have farm adventures riding four-wheelers, exploring the dump and finding collectibles, playing with stray kittens, visiting the cow graveyard, riding motorbikes and making jumps; we got up to all sorts of mischief! I enjoyed physical activities but wore really girly clothes. I was a pink-wearing tomboy in an environment that let my imagination run wild. I will always remember how magical childhood felt: colourful, full of excitement and completely enchanting.

ACTING

I was always interested in acting and knew I wanted to be a performer of some kind. My singing voice was mediocre and my dance skills needed some serious polishing, so I decided to try out acting and it seemed to flow quite easily. I signed with a local acting agency and started doing some background work (I was an extra in *Wolf Creek* – the pool party scene!) and then I got offered a film called *2:37*, about youth suicide. The director, Murali K. Thalluri, saw my headshot and decided he wanted to meet me. We met in the city and shared a love for Michael Jackson. Funnily, it was that connection that saw him hire me for his film! The film was shot on a micro budget and we were lucky enough that it went on to premiere in the 'Un Certain Regard' section at the Cannes Film Festival in 2006. Having a first film premiere at Cannes is like winning the golden ticket in a Willy Wonka bar!

THE CHALLENGES

Each role is challenging in some way. Sometimes it's learning a new skill, like preparing to be a jockey for the film *Ride Like a Girl*, or transforming into a rowing star for *A Discovery Of Witches*. Other times the challenge is in the lifestyle. We can never make long-term plans and often have zero idea how our year will look as jobs pop up with sometimes as little as two weeks' notice. We miss our homes and friends when we are away from Adelaide and Los Angeles. The transient nature of this career is one of the most challenging yet most exciting aspects of it.

THE IMPACT OF SOCIAL MEDIA

In some ways social media is an amazing tool for self-expression and connecting with people you wouldn't necessarily get to meet in everyday life. I have made some beautiful friendships over social media and can always use it as a way to show gratitude to supporters who drive me to keep a job in the acting industry. It's wonderful in many ways but it can also be soul-sucking and addictive if we let it. I believe that having a healthy relationship with social media is key and limiting our usage is a good idea. That way we can enjoy it for all its perks but ensure that it doesn't lead us down a dark path of comparison or judgement.

YOUR ZEN LIFE

I have two websites, Your Zen Life (YZL) and Your Zen Mama (YZM). YZM is a space for parents and caregivers to have a voice, connect and share stories. I think we need more positive parenting communities out there where we celebrate what connects us rather than fixating on what divides us. We need to embrace, encourage, accept and inspire each other on our parenting journey. YZL is the sister site of YZM and is about wellness and living our best lives in a conscious and mindful manner. As part of YZL I do vlogs (video blogs) called 'Tez Talks'. I really wanted to start a conversation with our YZL community that felt open, candid and connected. My industry gives out such a false sense of reality, I wanted to strip away the smoke and mirrors, pull down the pedestal and just celebrate what's REAL. So I am unfiltered, honest, open and share my discomforts, lessons and experiences with my audience. It's been so well received that it inspired me to keep going! I love it when someone recognises me for Tez Talks rather than my movies.

THE JUGGLE

My industry is one that really supports the working mother. I am often able to bring my kids to work with me, and my husband and I have supported each other's passions so that we could strike a healthy balance between our parenting and working lives. Mark will come to a country when I'm filming to take care of the kids and I'll take the kids to him when he is working.

Communication is fundamental and Mark and I communicate about everything. It's really important to remember that you and your spouse are the tree trunk and that the kids are the branches, which means that to be a strong family the trunk has to be healthy, strong and thriving. We also make sure we dedicate time to each other outside of our time with the kids.

CAREER HIGHLIGHT

My biggest career highlight has been attending the Oscars when *Hacksaw Ridge* was nominated. It was also my thirty-first birthday so it was extra special, a magical night that I will never forget!

MY BABIES

Meeting Bodhi was the most surreal feeling in the world; I could never find words to articulate it. He was this tiny little thing that made me a mother. I felt instantly bonded and in love with him, all my dreams had come true in that moment. With Forest, I was on an absolute high, as I already knew what it felt like to be a mother. I was crying with happiness when I pulled him out and onto my chest, and I just remember feeling completely at home with him. You just can't stop kissing and snuggling them, I didn't want to put either of them down and basically didn't for the first few months!

The challenges are numerous and it all depends on the week! They can come from navigating through a particularly challenging time for Bodhi due to a significant transition such as moving countries, Mark being away or if I go back to work after a period of being at home with him. Trying to problem-solve and figure out the best way to support him can be hard, especially when life is pulling you in all sorts of directions. Other times the challenge comes from dealing with my own feelings surrounding my boys being in any kind of suffering, such as getting hurt, being picked on, feeling left out, sad, afraid etc. There will always be moments when my sons are feeling big emotions of one kind or another but I just need to be accepting of all the life lessons they will learn, even if the thought of them having any kind of hardship is confronting for me.

Having children has changed every aspect of my life. All of my interactions, experiences and adventures are connected to my boys because the world is so much more vibrant now that they are in it. Every sensation, colour, feeling and moment is richer and deeper since becoming a mum. The frequency of the world has changed for me. I also see through the eyes of my boys so my perspective has changed. I've grown softer, more patient, my heart is fuller and I'm a more compassionate, understanding and loving person. I've also learned to survive on very little sleep!

Photographer Sam Elsom | Creative by Sheree Commerford of Captain And the Gypsy Kid

Photographer Sam Elsom | Creative by Sheree Commerford of Captain And the Gypsy Kid

FAMILY LIFE

We are avid board gamers in our family; we just love a good board game! You can often find us around the kitchen table playing Bingo, Uno, Monopoly, Cluedo, Mysterium, Key to the Kingdom, Race to the Treasure and more. Our whole family adores it! It's usually the first thing we do before we leave the house and the last activity we do before books and bedtime. We also love bike riding and often chuck the bikes in the car, park in a street and spend hours riding around as a family, going to parks, having picnics, eating great vegan food and spending the day together. We love it.

HEALTHY LIVING

I aim for a healthy balance at all times. I try to eat nutrient-dense foods and exercise as much as possible, but I also don't shy away from a packet of Gummy Bears or not exercising for a month! I've realised that being too regimented doesn't work for me. Being fluid, listening to my body and being in flow with myself means I have more longevity in terms of wellbeing. Mental wellbeing is the most important for me; sourcing happiness internally rather than externally is imperative to this. Reading, meditation and having time for reflection is a big part of my journey to a healthy mind.

THINGS THAT MAKE ME SMILE

Families: I love watching families interacting, brothers and sisters running around, mothers bonding with their children and watching the way they look at their kids. There is nothing I love more than celebrating the connection and power of a family.

Pregnant women: Seeing a round belly and a glowing mama-to-be makes me giddy with excitement for them, especially if they're about to become a first-time mother. It's an incredible time in a woman's life. We are such powerful and incredible creatures.

The love between my sons: Forest asking Bodhi for cuddles multiple times an hour! Bodhi taking such pride in his role as Forest's 'big brother helper', the way he always has Forest's back and helps him when he is in need. How they snuggle into each other for comfort and hold hands. To see these two blossoming in their brotherhood brings tears to my eyes. I'm so glad they will always have each other.

ROLE MODELS

There is no one person in particular that I look to as a role model – people inspire me all the time. I'm most taken by strong, amazing mothers balancing their own dreams and taking care of their families, while participating in ways to be the change they wish to see in the world. The women who aren't afraid to be real, vulnerable and mess up; the women who are committed to having vibrant, healthy and connected family lives; and the women who are always looking for ways to be of service to those in need. I believe women can do it all! I'm constantly in awe of my friends and the way they manage their lives.

SUCCESS IS …

Raising conscious-minded, happy children.

LESSONS FROM MY MOTHER

My mum always said that love is all you need (she was a big Beatles fan!). She is the most selfless, compassionate, giving and gentle person I have ever met in my life and I try to encompass all of those beautiful attributes that she taught me.

MOTHER ADVICE

To relax! Do less, be more, slow down. Meet the needs of your kids when they arise, don't try and force them into a schedule, just go with the flow and embrace the imperfection, the spontaneity and keeping it light!

HAPPINESS IS . . .

A home of full hearts, happy minds, healthy attitudes and a positive, connected spirit. Spending lazy Aussie days with my conscious-minded, loving community of best friends, with all of our children running around barefoot through the sprinklers, eating yummy vegan food, drinking delicious red wine, surrounded by nature and having deep, soul-reaching, inspiring conversations!

'Having children has changed every aspect of my life. All of my interactions, experiences and adventures are connected to my boys because the world is so much more vibrant now that they are in it.'

Photographer: Steve Wise

BIANCA RINEHART

MOTHER, WIFE, PHILANTHROPIST,
TRUSTEE OF THE HOPE MARGARET HANCOCK TRUST

'Becoming a mother absolutely changed my life. It's the most fulfilling role and I wouldn't change it for the world!'

I am acutely aware of how fortunate I am. I have an uncanny ability to see the positive in everything. I feel strongly about a number of issues and can't stay silent when something needs to be said. I see this as a strength. Others might find it irritating. I'm extremely appreciative of everything positive in my life, and learn from everything else. As with my pioneering ancestors, Pilbara red blood runs through my veins. I was proudly part of the opening crew at the Hope Downs mine, driving 240-tonne Komatsu trucks, setting up the pit, waste-dump layout etc. I think I was the only person on the FIFO plane more excited flying up to the Pilbara than back down to Perth again at the end of our week-long shifts.

The 5 a.m. starts, twelve-hour workdays, dust, heat and flies didn't worry me at all. I'd been kicking around in that ochre-red iron-rich dust all my life and loved it. Although the Pilbara of my childhood was very different to the Pilbara today.

We rarely encountered another person (and never their trash) and were able to enjoy the beautiful, pristine gorges all to ourselves. I have to say that although I miss the good old days, I'm immensely proud of my grandfather's foresight and determination in developing the area. Enabling it to become the employment and government revenue powerhouse it is today. It was no easy feat – at the time of my grandfather's discoveries few believed him that the iron was there. He had to lobby to have embargos lifted and brought in Rio Tinto, negotiating a royalty for his discoveries while also securing his own iron-rich land that has grown our family company into what it is today. Now the Pilbara is the largest iron ore producer and exporter in the world. I wish Lang could be here to see it. We certainly felt his presence as we celebrated my brother's wedding in Karijini Park a few years ago.

GIVING BACK

While working through some confronting personal issues in London in my teens, I wanted to take the focus off

'What we need in the world is more compassion, and more people wanting to ease the pain of others rather than inflicting it onto them.'

Photographer: Steve Wise

myself a little, to experience life from other viewpoints.

One of the volunteer roles I took on at this time was at a school for children with cerebral palsy, helping mostly with their hydrotherapy sessions. There was one particular young boy I worked with who, given his disability, was restricted in terms of mobility, requiring help getting dressed, eating and other tasks we able-bodied take for granted. But as soon as he was in the water, he was determined to make a length of the pool unassisted. Week after week he put in his best effort. The determination and heart that child displayed, despite his disability, stuck with me forever. I feel this experience of taking the focus off myself, through giving back to the community, in particular to those less fortunate, enabled me to see past my own pain at that time, put my troubles into perspective and led to my passion for 'giving back'.

I truly feel that the more you give, the lighter your load. Giving isn't just about monetary amounts, it has to come from the heart, and not with expectations of receiving something in return. What we need in the world is more compassion and more people wanting to ease the pain of others rather than inflicting it on them.

In terms of charitable interests, I've worked with orphanages in China and Thailand, became a founding director of Dreamfit (a West Australian organisation aimed at improving the lives of those with disabilities), continue to be involved with breast cancer charities, environmental and endangered wildlife initiatives, and help with other causes as and where I can.

However I am most acutely passionate about children. In particular, ensuring abused or neglected children can access early support and care. I believe this is a critical area, as addressing this trauma early can be a circuit breaker and put the child on a healthier life path than where they might have otherwise been headed without this positive intervention.

At thirteen I was fortunate to find a home at Bertha Bailey House, a small dormitory with a nurturing, family feel at Phillips Academy in Andover, Massachusetts. My dorm mother, Rebecca Sykes, is now President of Oprah Winfrey's charitable foundation, and runs the OWLAG Academy in South Africa. The respect and admiration I have for Oprah and Rebecca, and the work they are doing is off the charts. I feel this appointment is a match made in heaven! Both these women are truly inspirational to me.

Locally in Australia, I am very fortunate to have a dear friend in Ros Worthington, who is one of the most selfless, tireless, impassioned philanthropists I have ever met. And my grandmother, Hope Hancock (née Nicholas – our son's namesake) was renowned for her kind and generous nature and active philanthropy. I support her philosophy of a well-lived or successful life, which is: 'If you are doing something useful and you enjoy doing it, that's the essence of life.'

FAMILY

It was very special for me to have our son experience the Pilbara with his cousins. He's half-Australian and half-Russian, and proud of both sides! However Sash and I have brought him up in a way where it's obvious he's happier out in the bush than he would be on the streets of Moscow. We are very much a kookaburras, campfires and stars in the night sky family over the bright lights, big city, siren type. Nicholas is a very bright boy but we believe in addition to school, it's equally important to spend time off the grid, to get an appreciation for what otherwise might be taken for granted. It's very important to me that he is able to appreciate how fortunate he is. We have travelled as a family quite extensively through rural China, which is a place that has always captivated me. Nicholas was able to see children his age, working, manning the street-side stall of their family's citrus farm. He has played with local village children who are likely to have rarely received many presents in their lives. It warms my heart that he always cares deeply for others. Whether it be people or animals, he stands up to any cruelty or bullying on behalf of others, which makes me so proud. We also love going on hiking holidays as a family. Some of our favourite hiking destinations include Cradle Mountain in Tasmania, British Columbia in Canada and Yangshuo, China.

CLEAN LIVING

In addition to optimising our time outdoors, we tend to eat very clean – we are big fans of locally sourced, organic (where possible) fruit and vegetables. I don't eat meat and rarely if ever drink any alcohol – I feel my system can't handle either and I am happy to go without both! We as a family don't consume any dairy and also avoid gluten. However I love fish, especially if it's freshly caught by my husband! I also love essential oils and use them in the kitchen, laundry/cleaning and also make my

Photographer: Steve Wise

own deodorant with them. Anything that provides a more proactive and natural approach to health is something I'm happy to explore! I'm very anti-plastic in terms of its impact on both our health and the planet's, so limit its use in our home. We have also been against excessive screen time for Nicholas. I find it so sad that kids these days grow up with the adults around them so frequently staring at their phones. We make sure to put ours down for meals and other important quality times such as listening to Nicholas tell us about his day at school. Kids shouldn't be made to feel like they have to compete with technology. Although it's often because of the technology that we are able to spend more time with our kids, it's still important to make that quality time, not filtered through a distracting phone screen.

THE JUGGLE

As for most people, it can be a struggle to balance passions while leaving enough time for family and other personal commitments. Especially for me given if I take on a role, I want very much to deliver. Whereas before having our son I was happy to set substantial personal time aside for board meetings, functions and fundraising, I now loathe being away from my family so have to think long and hard before taking on any official role, preferring to help in more flexible, behind-the-scenes ways. I don't want to miss anything when it comes to my son.

Becoming a mother absolutely changed my life. It's the most fulfilling role and I wouldn't change it for the world!

'I now loathe being away from my family. I don't want to miss anything when it comes to my son.'

MEGAN GALE

MODEL, ACTRESS, BUSINESSWOMAN, MUM

'Meeting my children for the first time was the most precious, special, beautiful, heart-warming, impactful moment of my life. I was just awestruck and both moments were so special in their own way.'

I had a relatively normal and typical childhood growing up in Perth. What I remember is how I used to pass the time and make up my own little games. I was quite independent being the only girl and a bit younger than my brothers. I guess I was what you would've called (back then) a little bit of a mix of a 'tomboy' and a 'girly girl', in that I split my time either playing with dolls or mucking around in the dirt looking for bugs and following my brothers around. Now that I think about it from a parent's perspective and having both a son and a daughter, I always try to encourage just general fluid play, without activities being assigned to 'boys' things and 'girls' things. It was great that, even back then, I was allowed to play freely in whatever activity consumed my attention and that my parents encouraged this.

CAREER SUCCESS

My transition into various roles and stages of my career has always progressed naturally and organically. There was, needless to say, a lot of hard work put in over the years to get to certain stages of my career but I guess in terms of transitioning into different roles, I was lucky that the right opportunities presented themselves to me, always at the right time. They were all things that I had a keen interest in prior to doing them, i.e. acting, television presenting, design and so on, and they've all been jobs that have helped me grow, understand more about myself and learn so, so much about life in general. I think that that has been one of the biggest gifts of having such a diverse career.

Of course there have been a few challenges. One challenge I think even to this day I'm still navigating through is losing my anonymity. It happened so swiftly to me, without warning and without any conscious effort on my part that it really caught me unaware. Being such a naturally private and reserved person probably contributed to me not handling it too well. I know it must

seem like a silly thing to call a 'challenge' but we all have our strengths and weaknesses, and I guess you can't ever really know what it's like to be put under a microscope until it happens to you. The other challenge for me has been working through trust issues. A lot of people that I've worked with have abused my trust over the years and I have been taken advantage of multiple times, despite my best efforts to protect myself, and it has had a lasting impact on me. But you have to try and learn from these incidents as best you can and move onwards and upwards.

MEETING RIVER AND ROSIE

Meeting them both for the first time. . . ahhh… the most precious, special, beautiful, heart-warming, impactful moment of my life. I was just awe-struck and both moments were so special in their own way. River being our first baby, of course it was just so special and such a new experience for us. With Rosie, being a girl and knowing that we were having a daughter second time around and after a miscarriage, was very special too. But also, seeing River and Rosie meet for the first time – our hearts just exploded!

THE JUGGLE

The biggest challenge has been the juggle and finding that balance! Trying to find enough hours in the day to work, spend quality time with both kids and fit in things like grocery shopping, cooking, housework etc. and, where you can, sneak in time with your partner and for yourself. Some days the balance doesn't quite happen but we are so lucky to have our mums around to help out which allows us to be working parents too, but there is still so much to do every day! It's challenging but it's doable and my god there are parents out there who are doing it tougher than us and that puts it all into perspective. I think I always knew that I would have children a little later in life. I guess I half factored that into my career plan, in that I worked hard to achieve a lot of goals prior to having children, knowing that I would want to take as much time off as I could to be with them, especially in those earlier months. Both Shaun and I are lucky as well, in that while we have busy jobs, they are not Monday to Friday nine to five, and there is a little flexibility there with our respective schedules.

I guess our priorities have completely changed: it is all about the kids first and foremost. But that being said, and again I can't stress this enough, it's all about a careful balance and that is how you can best manage the juggling act. I believe that it is crucial to try, where possible, to allow for a little time to yourselves as parents, both individually and together. We tend to lose a little (sometimes a large) part of ourselves as we become parents, and it can happen without you even realising it. If you can manage it among the crazy, keep checking in with yourself and with your partner, and every now and then make that time for a date night or a massage or whatever is going to allow you to reclaim a little bit of you, and make sure it's guilt free! It takes a little while to learn how to do this and do it guilt free, but I feel this makes a big difference to my headspace and it ultimately makes me feel like I can be a better parent and give more of myself overall.

FAMILY LIFE

It's pretty busy during the day and every day is different depending on which one of us is working and who has the kids. Throughout the weekend and when we have days off during the week, we like finding new and different parks to play at with the kids, going for long drives and walks, and visiting places like the zoo or the aquarium. But every night, usually without fail, 4–7 p.m. is always family time. This consists of lots of games, playtime and reading books. Usually anything work-related – phones, computers and emails – all get put to the side and it's about us as a family. It's hectic, chaotic and crazy in our house during that window, but at the same time we have our routine and it works very well for us.

'We like finding new and different parks to play at with the kids, going for long drives and walks.'

SOCIAL MEDIA

I think social media has had a positive impact in some regard, but I think it's had a negative impact as well (this is purely my humble opinion of course!). On one hand I think it's great for businesses (especially small startups) as it gives them more of an interactive and broad reach for their brands. Socially, I think it's great as it allows you to stay frequently in touch with people in your life and gives an insight into what they've been up to in a way that you wouldn't normally see. It also allows you to get to know more about someone who would otherwise be simply an acquaintance – you can forge friendships in this way and also connect to new people. And I love that within your own account, you have your own voice and your own content, and this can be very empowering when it's needed. However, social media can be highly addictive. So much so that now, more than ever, it seems we spend so much time glued to the screens of our phones. Social media has definitely contributed to that addiction and increased time spent procrastinating. I'm not perfect by any means, far from it, but I always try to make a conscious effort to regularly take time away from social media (and my devices) and to especially not let it impact on the quality time I want to spend with my loved ones – I don't want to be living my life through my phone. It's great to indulge in, but like most things, it's about finding that careful balance.

HEALTH AND WELLBEING

For me I really thrive when I'm in balance. Finding a perfect balance usually requires maintaining optimum health of both the mind and the body. For my body, this requires a healthy and balanced diet, adequate exercise and the right type of exercise too. I listen to my body and respect how it wants to move that day, and I always try not to push myself in a direction I don't want to go in physically. And for my mind, I think this requires maintaining manageable stress levels, getting enough sleep and letting go of the things that don't serve me. All easier said than done, of course, but they are some good guidelines I try my best to live by in order to maintain that optimum health and wellbeing balance.

THINGS THAT MAKE ME SMILE . . .

The sight and sound of my children laughing, especially when it's together and at each other; a swim in the ocean on a hot summer's day; and my partner's sense of humour.

MY ROLE MODEL IS . . .

It sounds like a bit of a cliché but my mum. She is the queen of finding balance, calm and clarity in the most chaotic of situations. She taught me so, so much and there are so many of her life lessons that I'm still trying to perfect the practice of, but she has always been big on not sweating the small stuff, keeping things in perspective, living in the present moment (especially when it comes to your children) and not getting bogged down with the past or the future. She's a wise woman.

BEST MUM ADVICE

The best advice I've been given as a mum is to enjoy your children and their company as much as you can while they're young, as they grow up so fast. For this reason, I try to spend as much quality time with them as possible and be totally present with them.

HAPPINESS IS . . .

I've always loved the saying 'health is wealth.' When my loved ones and I are healthy and thriving then happiness tends to follow.

LISA WILKINSON

TELEVISION HOST *THE PROJECT*, JOURNALIST, MOTHER OF THREE

'Without question, our greatest achievement has been making a family together with three incredible children. Nothing else comes close.'

MY CHILDHOOD

I am blessed. My childhood was idyllic and utterly uncomplicated. I grew up in Campbelltown in Sydney's outer south west suburbs in a very traditional household, on a street that wound its way into beautiful Australian bushland. We were two brothers, a hard-working dad who was very involved in the local community, a stay-at-home mum and me. I walked to school every day, rode my bike, climbed trees, played street cricket until it was dark with all the kids in our neighbourhood, went to ballet classes and attended the local public school. I remember bonfires in the backyard on cracker night, Sunday School picnics and swinging on ropes before doing 'bombs' when we went swimming at the local river called The Woolwash. They say if you remember sunny days when you think of your childhood, it was a good one. And I can only think of sun streaming through every inch of my young life.

HOW I STARTED MY CAREER IN JOURNALISM

I had finished Year 12 and a year-long secretarial course, when I answered a tiny three-line ad in the Women & Girls Employment section of the *Sydney Morning Herald*. It read; '*Dolly Magazine* is looking for a secretary/editorial assistant/Girl Friday who is prepared to do absolutely anything. Phone Kathy on 6993622. And I did phone Kathy. I had read *Dolly* for all of my teenage years, so I couldn't believe it when I saw the ad. And to this day it is still the only job I have ever applied for. I knew I wanted to be a journalist, and soaked up every aspect of it. I worked so hard that six months after I started they gave me a cadetship. Eighteen months after that I became the editor – a perfect collision of hard work, right-place-right-time and something I can't recommend highly enough – finding your passion.

WHAT IT WAS LIKE BEING AN EDITOR AT 21

There was no one more surprised than me when I was offered the job. And I just knew that there were fully-trained up journalists right throughout the company thinking 'Who the hell does this trumped up little typist think she is?' Truth is, I was thinking exactly the same thing. So I had to ignore the naysayers, work hard, listen to my gut instincts about what was right for the magazine and its readers, surround myself with the most talented people I could find, and be honest with all of my staff and admit that I was on a massive learning curve. In fact, being thrust into this role so quickly, nobody had got around to teaching me any of the rules. So I wrote a few of my own . . . and probably broke plenty. I wanted to change things up a bit, challenge the norms, treat the readers with more maturity, give the magazine more depth, tackle issues that I felt were important to them but hadn't been dealt with in the magazine before. As well as all the fashion and fun, I wanted to be sure that I used this position and influence I had been so privileged to be given, wisely. I believed very strongly that knowledge was power, particularly for teenage girls. And it was also during this time – a time when blonde-haired, blue-eyed Aussie surfie chicks ruled – that I gave a totally unknown fifteen-year-old corkscrew-curled redhead not only her first moment in front of the camera, but also her very first magazine cover. It was July 1983, and in the years since she's done quite well. In fact, by some estimates she has appeared on around 30,000 magazine covers since. She was, of course, Nicole Kidman. Fortunately my strategy worked, because four years after I took over at *Dolly*, we had tripled the magazine's circulation. I worked bloody hard, but I loved every minute of it.

HOW DID PRINT TO TV HAPPEN?

I was on maternity leave after spending ten years as editor of *Cleo*, and I got a call from an old mate in PR, Brian Walsh, who was now running the newly launched Foxtel pay TV service. He wanted to start up the next incarnation of a panel show called *Beauty and the Beast* – a show my mum used to watch when I was a kid – and he wanted me to be a regular panellist. Now, I'd been interviewed on TV plenty of times over the years, but I'd never done anything straight down the barrel of the camera. But I figured I'd give it a go. After all, I was a magazine person and this was just a bit of fun on the side. I could have a go at learning a new skill, challenge myself a little . . . but it was TV so I never thought of it as any sort of serious career move. I'll never forget Brian coming down to the studio floor on that very first day, and there I was sitting on the panel next to TV royalty like Jeanne Little, Ita Buttrose and a former long-time morning show host and Miss Australia called Maureen Duval. While they were all happily chatting and raring to go, I was sitting there like a rabbit caught in the searing glare of headlights on full beam. At that point Brian leaned in and whispered to me, 'What the hell's the matter with you?' before I reminded him that I'd never done this sort of thing before. And his response was something I have carried with me every day since as I make my living in this strange, often ego-driven, altered TV universe: 'Oh for heaven's sake, get over yourself, it's only television!'

GREATEST ACHIEVEMENT

I think probably keeping grounded and my head screwed on enough in my professional life to know that it is my personal life that is the most important. It has always been my priority and I feel so blessed to have met in my husband a man who has only amplified that feeling. Without question, our greatest achievement has been making a family together with three incredible children. Nothing else comes close.

HAVING KIDS

The time when I was having my kids ended up becoming my transition years, when I started spreading my journalistic wings by going freelance and doing radio, newspapers and TV. Not being tied to a full-on one-job career made it easier to set up my own consultancy business and then pick and choose what I would do. It gave me the freedom to try new things. I figured I had nothing to lose and everything to gain, including experience in areas which I'd never worked in before. I could set my own hours, and it also gave me lots of precious time with my kids when they were little.

STRUGGLES FACED GOING BACK TO WORK

First and foremost, like every woman, the biggest struggle was getting good childcare. And second was that awful moment when I looked back at the full-time professional merry-go-round that I used to be on, and thinking that it seemed to be going a whole lot faster than when I got

'Be kind to yourself. This whole working mum caper doesn't come with a rule book.'

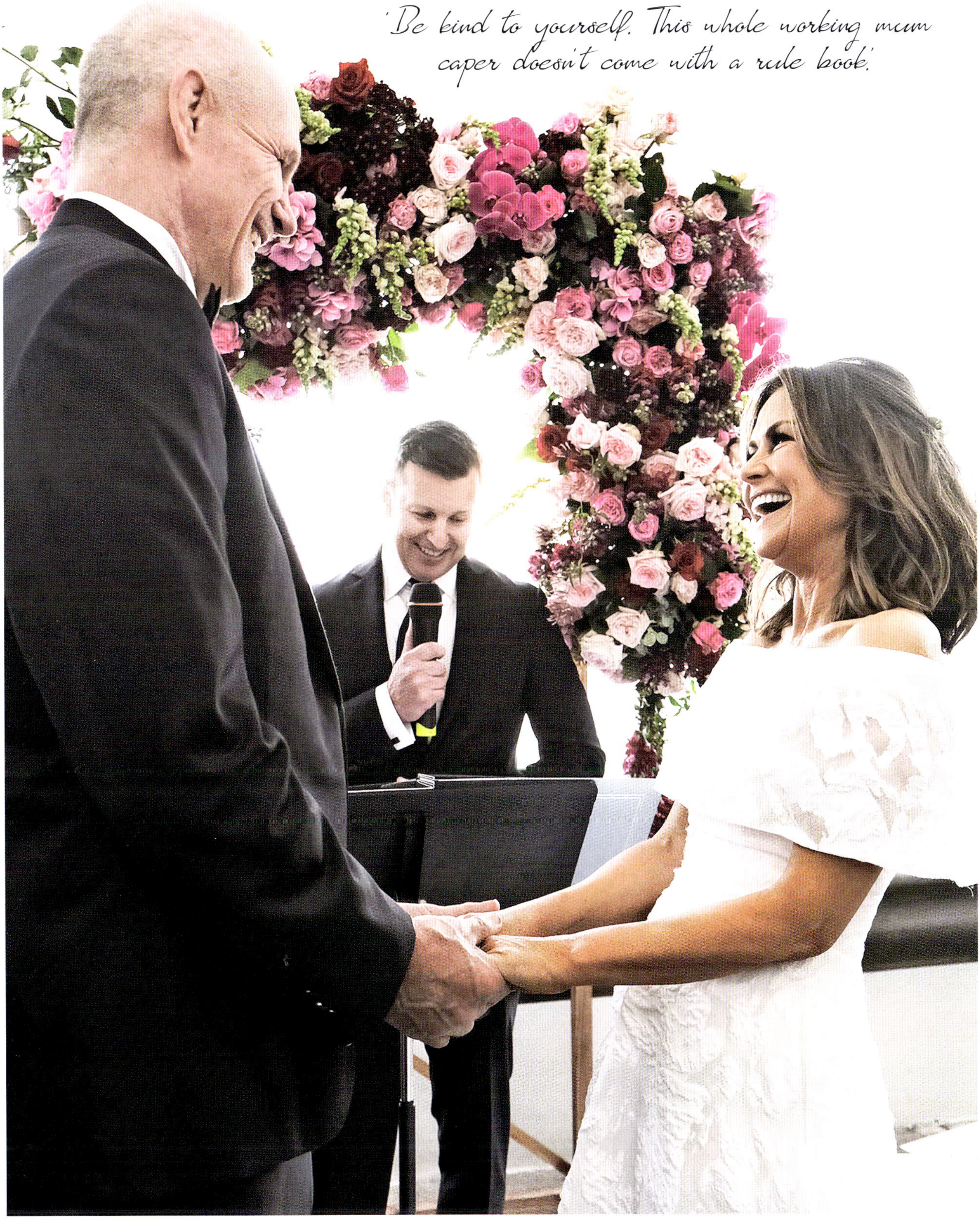

off. It wasn't. But there's something about having babies and taking time out from the professional world that can make you feel excluded, vulnerable and out of touch. The only way forward is to just jump back on. That's when you realise that you're not only just as capable, but you've also gained some much-needed perspective. And I have no doubt become a much better employee and journalist because of it.

HOW TOUGH WAS THE DECISION TO LEAVE *TODAY*?

Very tough. I will always be grateful for the privilege of that job, and for being welcomed into so many Australian homes and families' lives each and every morning. But it was something I had been contemplating for a while. I'd had ten and a half incredible years at *Today*, and become the show's longest-serving female host, which was such an honour. But while there was much about it I still loved, I felt I'd stopped learning. And I always promised myself that when that day came, it was time to move on. The opportunity to join *The Project*, work with and learn from a team I had long admired, as well as start doing more long-form journalism was just too good to refuse.

BEST PIECE OF ADVICE YOUR MOTHER GAVE YOU?

'Learn from your mistakes.' And I hope I have.

DO WE STILL HAVE A LONG WAY TO GO AS WOMEN?

Absolutely, but real change is happening, and personally I think it's never been a better time to be a woman. The Harvey Weinsteins of this world can run, but they can no longer hide. Because the truth is, we women ARE good enough. In fact, we are MORE than good enough. And we have to give ourselves permission to know that, to acknowledge that and to embrace that. But we have to hold hands, support each other and do this together.

HOW DO YOU PERSONALLY OVERCOME STRUGGLES OR SETBACKS?

I had a pretty awful time being bullied when I was in high school, and I will never forget walking out of those school gates on the day I finished my very last exam, and making a promise to myself that I would never again allow someone else to decide who I was, and what I was capable of. It gave me a strength and a resolve that has lasted all through my adult years. It also hasn't hurt being lucky enough, wise enough and patient enough to wait for my soul mate to come along: my husband. His support and belief in me always gives me the extra push that I sometimes need.

ADVICE TO OTHER WORKING MUMS

Be kind to yourself. This whole working-mum caper doesn't come with a rule book. It isn't easy. Our scenarios are all different and constantly changing. And trying to have it all – and do it all is guaranteed to end in tears. Don't be shy about looking for support in whatever way you need it, and to give yourself permission to get things wrong. It's advice I still give myself every day.

HAPPINESS TO ME IS. . .

Family, loyal friends, open fires, kindness, the innocence of children and the luxury of stillness.

THE MOST IMPORTANT JEWELS THAT WILL EVER BE WRAPPED AROUND YOUR NECK ARE THE ARMS OF YOUR CHILDREN.

PINK

SALLY OBERMEDER

TV HOST, BESTSELLING AUTHOR, FOUNDER OF SWIISH

'Without question, happiness for me is spending time with my family and friends. Honestly, nothing else in the world matters when I'm with them.'

I had a simple, suburban childhood. Both my parents worked as accountants until my sister, Maha, was born five years after me, then Mum stayed home to raise us. My parents didn't have any family around so it was just us. We were a close, tight-knit family and now Maha and I are extremely close. In an era of dads being more hands off than on, my dad was very different. He would always come to our netball games and be standing with all the mums cheering us on. My mum went back to work once I went to high school. She was a dynamic, strong role model for Maha and me.

CAREER PATH

I wanted to either be a dentist (funny, right?), or a TV presenter when I grew up. I wanted to be a dentist because I was obsessed with brushing my teeth but once I did work experience at a dental surgery, I realised I wouldn't like it because it's actually really hard to speak to the patients, considering they have their mouths open and can't talk! That cancelled that option out! I also wanted to be a TV presenter, and I'd sit and learn my notes for tests by pretending I was presenting the news. I would set up my desk as the news desk and put on what I thought was my 'news voice'. Mum would come in and ask me what I was doing, and I'd say back that I was reading my biology notes as if it was the 6 p.m. news. Tragic but true, ha!

Way, way before kids I worked in finance. Then at the age of thirty, I decided to have a career change. I decided I wanted to go for my dream of working in TV. So I spent the next few years learning, interning and doing whatever coaching and tuition I could to try and break into TV. While doing that, I worked as a personal trainer and Pilates instructor. After about three-and-a-half years of trying, I got my first proper TV job as a travel reporter and researcher.

Naturally life was easier before kids because we could

'I hope to teach my daughters resilience and kindness, because you can never have too much of either.'

spend more time on our careers and there was no one else for us to think about. Marcus and I had a decade together before Annabelle was born.

EXPANDING THE FAMILY

I was working at Channel Seven as the National Entertainment Reporter when I fell pregnant. I was interviewing movies stars, singers and celebs. It was hectic, fast-paced and I loved every minute of it. We worked long days under immense pressure to produce new content each day for the show, but it was a dream job and I relished every day.

MEETING ANNABELLE AND THE INSPIRATION THAT GOT ME THROUGH TOUGH TIMES

Meeting Annabelle for the first time was bittersweet. On the one hand I was overwhelmed with love for my baby girl, and on the other hand I so desperately feared I would not live long enough so see her live.

When Annabelle was a newborn and I had just been diagnosed with breast cancer, I honestly wouldn't have coped without my family and friends. They held me when I fell apart, they made me laugh, they loved and nurtured not just me but also Marcus and Annabelle. They organised a roster for meal deliveries and who would look after Annabelle while Marcus or Maha came with me to chemotherapy appointments. So as odd as it may sound, my inspiration during this time was gratitude. I'm grateful that I went through the cancer battle as it has given me a perspective and newfound outlook on life that I'm not sure I could have found any other way.

Cancer really makes you reassess what is important to you and what you need to do to live your best life. I now make sure I am always living in the present, always telling people I love them and always doing things that make me happy, rather than doing things I feel obliged to do.

HEALTH AND WELLNESS EMPIRE

After my cancer battle, I wanted to get well. Really well. I wanted to feel amazing. I wanted to feel good on the inside and out. I started making my own green smoothie recipes and then I got Maha onto it too. We saw the changes instantly. Better skin, improved digestion and more energy. We glowed. Everywhere we went people asked us for our recipes. So after months of scribbling down recipes for people, I had an idea to do a green smoothie recipe book. All the publishers said no, but we knew we had an excellent idea, so we decided to publish it ourselves. We created the recipes, photographed it in our kitchen and styled it all ourselves. We were totally committed.

We published it on iTunes and Amazon and it went to number one overnight. The publishers came back knocking. We published it as a paperback and it went on to become the number one bestselling smoothie book in Australia, and has since been republished about fifteen times including most recently in Polish.

At the same time we also started our website and online store: SWIISH.com. It's a feel-good site and we sell fashion, accessories, homewares and health products that are all about helping women nurture the inside and celebrate the outside. We have expanded our business and now under SWIISH WELLNESS, we proudly produce wellness products including our famous Super Green Superfood Powder, our Sleep Superfood Powder and our Collagen SuperSkin Powder.

The greatest joy for us is in the hundreds of messages we receive each day from women and men sharing with us how much better they feel and look, and how the products have literally changed their life for the better. Both Maha and I and our entire team, live for those messages.

MEETING ELYSSA

During the pregnancy with Elyssa I was working as a co-host on *The Daily Edition*, a live afternoon news and entertainment show at Channel Seven. I was also juggling that with SWIISH.com and working on the expanding range of SWIISH WELLNESS products, and new cookbooks. Planning for a second baby was much more hectic because we had Annabelle to run around after! It was a mixed experience, expecting Elyssa – on one hand it was nothing short of a miracle, but it was also a

hard experience because I wasn't carrying Elyssa myself, and I longed for that experience of carrying a baby again myself. But to have found a surrogate who was so, so incredible was the biggest blessing. The surrogacy journey was brilliant. I spoke to Rachel, our surrogate, all the time – she is amazing and we will have a bond for life. The long distance factor was definitely challenging, because I wasn't going to the appointments with her, so that was hard. Often, I would get up at 2 a.m. to be on a call when she was at an ultrasound. It was also challenging with Annabelle, because even though we talked about the pregnancy all the time and that her sibling was coming, it was still slightly out of mind out of sight. Whereas in a traditional pregnancy siblings get to see their mum's belly expand through the nine months and that is part of the adjustment process.

Meeting Elyssa was surreal. It was the most amazing feeling knowing that two families came together to ensure that this baby would arrive into the world, happy and healthy. Having Elyssa handed to me for skin-to-skin contact was unforgettable. It was also very raw watching Annabelle hold Elyssa for the first time, when she was just a few minutes old.

THE JUGGLE

Like most mums will tell you, your priorities change when you become a mum and I think you become a lot more selfless. All of a sudden, life isn't just about you! Every decision I make is now based on how it will impact Marcus, Annabelle and Elyssa, rather than just myself. I always thought I was an incredibly organised person but since becoming a mum of two, my organisation levels have gone up to the next level, which I didn't even think was possible. All my friends laugh at me because I'm so organised but I honestly wouldn't have it any other way. I have to be ridiculously organised to run my business, SWIISH.com with my sister, Maha Koraiem, be on television every day on *The Daily Edition* and be a wife and a mum to two beautiful girls. Although I'm no expert at juggling, I drop the ball all the time! Haha.

In terms of SWIISH, I'm incredibly proud of expanding the business, growing the team and expanding from just an idea into a product that does so much good for so many people. If I think of TV, I'm most proud to have worked so hard to take a dream to reality, with no contacts, no network and no experience at an age most people deemed 'too old to try a new career'.

I think honestly, there is no secret to the juggle. Generally no two days are the same, and often they don't go according to plan. There are some days when I think, 'urgh' today was a disaster'. And other days I'm like, 'woohoo, I'm a rockstar, I didn't drop the ball!' Haha. The one thing I do is I stay organised, I stay calm and I remind myself there are worse things than dropping the ball. As long as everyone is healthy then the rest can all get worked out.

MUM MOMENTS

I went through a period after Elyssa was born when I was up all night and I was really tired and not only was I not taking care of myself, but I wasn't asking for any help. I got so run down that I got an infection and my eardrum burst, and it was only when I had blood pouring out of my ear, that I realised I probably should have put my hand up and asked for help. Even I – someone who knows the importance of good health – sometimes still struggles with asking for help and accepting when I need to take a break.

Being a mum makes that harder because you feel like you have to be there for everyone but it's funny because as soon as you take a break and have some sleep and nurture yourself, you're better for everyone. There's no way you're going to go the distance without looking after yourself, and as someone very wise recently told me, it's a marathon, not a sprint.

APPROACH TO HEALTH AND FITNESS

'Small things make a big difference' is my motto. I have my Super Green Superfood Powder in the morning to get my green shot of goodness and get my body fired up. I have my Collagen Powder in my coffee to give my skin a hit of glow and I take my Sleep Powder at night. Three small things, but they tick three big boxes. I do those and I know I'm giving myself the best kind of self care there is.

LESSONS TO TEACH MY DAUGHTERS

I hope to teach my daughters resilience and kindness, as you can never have too much of either. I always say 'err on the side of humanity' – that way you can't go wrong.

HAPPINESS IS . . .

Without question, happiness for me is spending time with my family and friends. Honestly, nothing else in the world matters when I'm with them.

Photographer: Mackenzie Hunkin

LOUISE ROE

INTERNATIONAL TELEVISION HOST, JOURNALIST, AUTHOR, MOTHER

'My childhood was wonderful. We lived in the countryside outside of London, and my happiest memories are horse riding across this little river in the summer.'

Starting out in my career, I began an internship at *Elle* magazine right after graduating from uni, which was amazing! After months of photocopying and getting coffee, I was sent down to London Fashion Week where I went backstage and interviewed Linda Evangelista! It was a pinch-me moment I'll never forget. A few years later I moved out to Los Angeles and was lucky enough to host a makeover show called *Plain Jane*. That took off and we filmed five series all over the world, helping young women find their confidence (and great outfits too!). Funnily enough, I met my husband, Mackenzie, on *Plain Jane* as he was the director. After that I started hosting awards show red carpets and fashion segments for *Access Hollywood*, a morning show on NBC. I still work with them and it's a real buzz when awards season comes around.

My biggest career highlight has been hosting the Oscars red carpet live in front of thirty-one million people! I have never been so nervous but it was awesome. I ended the show by racing from the red carpet to the actual Oscars stage in a golf cart, and did my last interview behind the theatre curtains as they counted down the final seconds to the show.

TWO BECOMES THREE

It's hard to put into words what it was like meeting my baby, but all the sayings you've heard new parents say, such as having never felt a greater love and overwhelming joy, are poignantly true. You're also physically exhausted, full of adrenaline and oxytocin and whatever else, so it's a huge, surreal high. I cried and felt very proud of Honor, as if the whole journey and effort of pregnancy – and labour – was very much shared between us.

THE JUGGLE

I actually found pregnancy harder in many ways than being a first-time mother. I felt very sick for my first and third trimesters, and not being able to work out, eat or

Photographer: Mackenzie Hunkin

'Every mother is trying to juggle it all and find the right balance, but really – if you can get it for a day, or an afternoon – that's great. You'll never get it for longer than that so stop trying. Just do your best and try not to be so hard on yourself.'

drink what I wanted, or stay up later than 9 p.m. without turning into a zombie. . . I found that difficult. But once you see the fruits of your labour (literally!) and you have a little person making you laugh and smile all day long, any difficulties are offset and balanced by that. It's definitely difficult balancing work and motherhood, especially as Mackenzie and I run our own company, so I didn't get any official maternity leave. Of course, not sleeping is a challenge, and means I can't be so spontaneous anymore. But in all honesty, these were challenges I was expecting, and they're the same for any other parent. It's what you sign up for!

I went back to work with mixed emotions, really polar emotions! I hosted the Oscars red carpet when Honor was six weeks old. I was full of adrenaline and excited to get back out there and use my brain. But I was also nervous, finding a dress was tricky as my body wasn't the same and I was nursing – so I needed breast pads and I pumped through hair and make-up – ahh the glamour! I also felt very guilty because it was the first time I'd left her all day. But my parents and husband were there looking after Honor, and I wonder if she one day will be proud of me for doing it. I hope so.

The biggest challenge for me has been breastfeeding. It is a wonderful, bonding experience and I feel lucky to have been able to do it. But the consistency (every two hours, twenty-four hours a day when they are born!) is a lot. I went to Italy for forty-eight hours when Honor was three months old. My hormones were all over the place and I had to pump in the plane loo over and over, and try to sanitize it all in this tiny Italian hotel room. For me that was hard. But worth it.

My friend put it really well the other day; she said balance is fleeting. Every mother is trying to juggle it all and find the right balance, but really – if you can get it for a day, or an afternoon – that's great. You'll never get it for longer than that so stop trying. Just do your best and try not to be so hard on yourself. But it goes without saying that family comes first, before anything. That has meant turning down jobs and trips, which is absolutely fine.

My advice for other working mums would be to be in touch with other working mothers. There are lots of websites and apps nowadays that help you meet them in your community. It really does help with advice and support.

FAMILY LIFE

We love to head out early on the weekend, grab coffees and go on a long walk around the neighbourhood. And I can't wait to take Honor to the beach for the first time! I was just on a long plane ride on my own, and got really inspired to write out some advice for our daughter. I hope she is kind to others, I hope she is confident enough to speak up when she sees something that isn't right, and I hope we have a close enough relationship that she'll always trust us and vice versa.

THINGS I LIVE BY

My mother taught me some things that are really important; that being heard doesn't mean shouting. To be at peace with spending time alone, and in fact, to really recharge from it. And that it's better to have fewer, really close friendships, than lots of fair-weather ones. The best advice I have ever been given as a mother is not to rush to the next milestone, soak up every minute and enjoy even the sleepless nights, because they grow so fast it will be over in a flash. And buy a special bra to pump with, it's a game changer!

THREE THINGS THAT MAKE ME SMILE. . .

Honor's giggle, old movies, skiing.

MY ROLE MODELS ARE . . .

An author called Tasmina Perry who gave me my first job and is still a great friend. My mum, who I adore so much. Amal Clooney kicks some serious ass in all areas.

HAPPINESS IS . . .

A glass of rosé by the BBQ in our back garden, music on, sun shining, friends and family jumping in the pool.

'Don't rush to the next milestone, soak up every minute and enjoy the sleepless nights, because they grow up so fast it will be over in a flash.'

Photographer: Mackenzie Hunkin

ERICA BARTLE

COMMUNICATIONS DIRECTOR FOR OUTLAND DENIM, MUM OF TWO

Outland Denim is the Australian jeans company changing the lives of young women in Cambodia through its profit-for-purpose business model. The company began as a means to create employment opportunities for young women affected by sex trafficking, emerging from NGO after-care programs. The business has since developed to offer a more inclusive business model offering training, employment, living wages and personal development initiatives to people of varying vulnerabilities, including those with disabilities.

'Meeting my baby for the first time was like life had just begun. I had never felt so alive.'

My childhood was a typical suburban childhood for a kid growing up in Brisbane in the 1980s; bike riding or roller-skating around the streets, swimming in the pool until my hands turned pruney, ballet lessons after school and on Saturday mornings, hanging out at neighbours' places, the smell of freshly cut grass after my dad mowed the lawn, Judy Bloom books borrowed from the library, Kylie Minogue on cassette tape, mangoes, watermelons and Rice Bubbles for eating, and Strawberry Quick mixed with milk slurped down for afternoon tea with a Milk Arrowroot biscuit. On the flip side, I was a chronic asthmatic, so I spent a lot of time off school in hospital. That wasn't so great. It was quite lonely. My parents divorced when I was in my first year of high school. That was a difficult time also.

THE CREATION OF OUTLAND DENIM

My husband and I saw the movie *Taken* with our best friends around 2009. He and his mate were pretty stirred by what they saw and read in the closing credits; the idea that this sort of thing (human trafficking) was actually happening and on a vast scale globally. We were at a music festival together a couple of years later when he had the opportunity to connect with an NGO doing work in that field. They persuaded him to go to Thailand and Cambodia to see the work they were doing with trafficking victims there. He was particularly moved by the sight of a very young girl prostituting herself on the streets and the feeling of helplessness never left him. He was incentivised to do something to help, but couldn't picture himself being the hero literally saving these girls. As we learned, it's not a black and white issue; it's extremely complicated.

My job as a journalist, his wife and supporter has been to unpack that and to help steer him around research, policy and communications implementation.

After five years getting our training and employment model, as well as our production to the scale, quality and legitimacy needed, we were finally ready to launch. That happened in 2016. But I have only ever played the best supporting role, and actually often play the devil's advocate: at every turn along the way he has had his wife asking, 'But can we do it this way? Or that way?' which

'My husband and I saw the movie 'Taken' with our best friends around 2009. He and his mate were pretty stirred by what they saw and read in the closing credits, the idea that human trafficking was actually happening and on a vast scale globally.'

must have been incredibly irritating. But also I believe we are better and stronger as a team; in areas where he is weak, I'm strong – vice versa.

THE MISSION

One of the most important things for women who have experienced sexual exploitation in particular, is to have somewhere to go and something to do once they have been through an aftercare program that helps them get back on their feet. Some of them have severe trauma and PTSD; some carry shame and stigma – no one suffers in the same way. But all of them need employment, as poverty is often the root cause of their being trafficked in the first place. Some of these young girls (and some are really, really young) have been encouraged to go to the cities or migrate across borders in search of work to support their families, and they wind up in hideous situations. Some have been raped close to home, and, for whatever reason, they have needed to be pulled out of that environment for sheer survival's sake, though if at all possible it is usually always the intention of the NGO to reintegrate the girl into her community and her family. So what we were trying to offer these young women with these awful histories of exploitation and abuse, is a socially protective mechanism to build their future through work and skills acquisition.

It has been a completely human-centric business model from the get-go. The jeans came second. But over time we have learned that without a product of a quality that can be marketed and sold on a global scale, we cannot be sustainable or make the impact that we desire. So we have worked extremely hard on our production standards and our product development.

THE DUCHESS OF SUSSEX

We were given the opportunity to present the royal couple with a modest selection of jeans prior to their royal tour Down Under, and it was extremely good timing.

It truly has been remarkable to see our brand name splashed across titles like *Vogue*, *Elle*, *Harper's Bazaar*, *WWD* and *Who What Wear*; this is where you see prestige and premium fashion brand names, and there we are with our name in the spotlight right alongside them. We have experienced an extraordinary amount of favour from the media, from customers, from retailers and from our community since Meghan wore our jeans on that now historic day in Dubbo, New South Wales.

THE MARKLE EFFECT

The interest has been global, vast and fast, so I imagine you will soon be seeing Outland Denim in some major retail establishments, as well as online globally. We are stocked in premium department stores in Canada such as Holt Renfrew and Harry Rosen, and we anticipate the same happening in Australia, the UK and the United States in time. The denim game is extremely competitive, especially at a premium level, but what we are offering is quite unique – the premium product but also the sound ethics and the sustainability element. Hopefully this major boost to our brand presence in the mind of media and people around the world will help us to achieve more of our mission in a shorter period of time. We have already seen this occur with fifteen new seamstresses able to be employed in the aftermath of the Markle Effect.

OUR LITTLE FAMILY

Meeting my baby for the first time was like life had just begun. I had never felt so alive. The second Isabel entered the world she was whisked away from me, as she was born seven-and-a-half weeks early. I didn't get to hold my baby to my chest like I had anticipated or gaze at her for long. As the private hospital where we had her couldn't accommodate premature babies, and they had mentioned the word 'abnormalities' after seeing her, we had to transfer. I had to quickly shower, dress and hop into the car to chase our baby, who was in an ambulance, to the public hospital a few suburbs away. We were absolutely beside ourselves. What just happened? Would she be okay? Where is our baby?! We ran from the car into the Neonatal Intensive Care Unit (NIC) and located her tiny little self in

the emergency area. 'Is she going to be okay?' we asked a nurse. We were told that she would be fine – apparently babies are born prematurely all the time! And as Isabel was thirty-two weeks and four days gestation, and not scarily early, she was going to be okay. We spent a month travelling to and from the hospital to visit our little baby, as they couldn't at the time accommodate parents sleeping overnight. We would race each other to her crib every morning. We were besotted. We would take turns giving her kangaroo cuddles for up to six hours at a time. We have been besotted since. I think we were very blessed in the sense that for a long time we doubted that we could have children, so to now have two beautiful, healthy little girls is our miracle.

THE JUGGLE

Before Isabel arrived I had decided to put down the tools, professionally speaking, and just be a mum. And, for the most part, that is what I did for the first three years of her life. It was wonderful. I did the occasional freelance project, but nothing that would require me to be away from her. I worked around her schedule. But then in September 2016, we launched Outland Denim. So I was back on deck part-time to see through the launch phase. I've been working on Outland in either a casual or part-time capacity since then, including after the birth of our second daughter, Emily, who would come to work with me as a baby. When she started walking around twelve months old, however, I really pulled back on my hours and tried to work only at night once the girls were in bed. As tough as those first two years are, and as taxing as working late into the night is, I wanted our bond to be as solid as mine and Isabel's had been.

During that time, we also moved to Cambodia for a few months so that James could oversee the next phase of our business, opening a new facility. I relished that time with both of the girls and saw them flourish as sisters also. So I would say that I have tried to be a mum first and foremost, and let my work with Outland revolve around that role. This is one of the blessings about working in your own business, and also within proximity to home and school, as we live within five to ten minutes of both.

I get to drop off and pick up Isabel from school most days, go to playgroup with Emily, and spend lots of lovely quality time with them, but then I also get to dip into my corporate brain as well. We chose not to use formal childcare and so have relied a lot on our 'village' to help with the children when needed – mostly the girls' grandmothers, but also my father, who lives next door, my sister-in-law, good friends and two exquisitely gorgeous young Outland staff who will take them out to afternoon tea or for a play at the park of their own accord, which has been lovely. These young women are good, strong role models for my girls; they're like surrogate aunts. In busy times for the business, I need to be more present with our team, but when things are quiet I really hone in at home.

THE CHALLENGES

My first experience of a newborn was really unusual – being introduced to the world of NICU. There were amazing nurses helping us to cope with our tiny premature baby, and we benefited greatly from their training – they taught us everything from how to change a nappy and cot sheets, to how to monitor our baby's heart rate, and how to breastfeed. I had access to the in-house lactation consultant and with the help of a breast pump, was finally able to breastfeed Isabel before she came home with us – one month after entering hospital. She fed until she was three, so we did well, but I don't know how I would have fared without that level of medical support. All mothers should have this – you need a village of women around you supporting and encouraging you as a new mum, especially in those sleep-deprived first few months. Neither of my babies have been good sleepers in the sense of sleeping through the night early, so that has been taxing, but that wakefulness totally prepared me for taking international PR calls during the night in a professional capacity.

My biggest challenge as a mum has been allowing others to help. I am a very independent and stubborn person. I think that I can do everything and do it the best! Of course I can't and I don't, so that journey through motherhood has been incredibly humbling. My pride has really gotten in the way at times of me asking for help and also receiving it; allowing others to share in the care of my children. I had this idea that I could be an incredibly dedicated mum, wife and homemaker, but as a perfectionist whenever I fell short of my imagined idea of what I should be achieving, I was a frustrated, anxious mess.

For a long time I also battled mother's guilt after I started working back in the business. I judged myself harshly for being unavailable to my little girl who really just wanted my complete, undivided attention and affection. In hindsight, I don't know that Isabel or I were ready for that step quite so early, but then if I hadn't made the transition back to work, I think all of her other transitions (to kindergarten and then school) away from me would have been much harder. Getting that balance right between being available to them and flexible to their needs, while also believing that you deserve to flourish in a personal

and professional capacity, is really difficult. I have definitely erred on the side of the martyr mother.

Some of the mothers I encountered in Cambodia would work in the city during the week and then go home to their babies at the weekend. I can't imagine having to physically work so far away from my children. I try to limit travel and cause as little upset to the girls' lives and routines as possible – I've been the lynchpin while their daddy travels extensively around the world in his role as CEO.

MY ROLE MODELS

I'm really blessed to live in a small community where some of the older women who've walked the road before me have taken me under their wing; some working mums, some full-time mums, but all just completely dedicated to their kids while doing interesting things in their own right despite the challenges. They push through. One of them is Sabine Bannard, an unassuming photographer from Germany who has shot for Outland Denim and was a DJ in a past life. She has created an amazing home with her husband, has two lovely teenaged children who actually like speaking to their mother, and some great credits under her belt after completely reinventing herself after having children in a new place. It is a long, hard road for some women to find this place of fulfilment but the reward is getting through and finding it, I think, not thinking you have to do it all before you are 30. That is so untrue.

MUM ADVICE

The best advice I've been given as a mother has been, 'Be the mother you are'. Sabine told me that very early on in my mothering journey. Of course, you don't want to be 'the mother you are' if you have some serious problems and yell at your children all day. But you do want your children to get a sense that you are an individual person with dreams, interests and capabilities that extend beyond the home, and not just a slave to their every whim. You will be the mother that you were created to be, bringing all your unique insight and personality into the mix of your role. Motherhood is a lot about self-acceptance. Your children will show you things about yourself that sometimes you wish they wouldn't. They are like a mirror of your attitudes and behaviour. So you might as well enjoy being yourself, deal with any hindrances to your flourishing as a human being, and teach them how to, as well!

THINGS THAT MAKE ME SMILE . . .

The beaming faces of my little girls when I pick them up after a period of separation during the day, watching my (divorced) parents enjoy their grandchildren individually or together, and listening to the girls giggle hysterically when they rough-play with their daddy.

MY PROUDEST ACHIEVEMENT IS . . .

My two girls! And working alongside my husband to make Outland Denim a viable, world-changing enterprise for some very special but disadvantaged women.

SUCCESS IS . . .

Success to me is knowing your limitations, knowing your value, knowing your responsibilities and also your vulnerabilities, and putting boundaries in place to ensure that you and those whom you love the most benefit from those things you choose to invest your time, talents and money into. If someone has to suffer so that you can get ahead, whether that be your children or your husband or your parents or friends, then I think you have to question the real validity or worth of that success.

MOTHERHOOD HAS A VERY HUMANISING EFFECT. EVERYTHING GETS REDUCED TO THE ESSENTIALS.

MERYL STREEP

Photography by Andrew Finlayson, The Australian Women's Weekly, Bauer Media Australia

NATALIE BARR

SUNRISE NEWSREADER, JOURNALIST, MUM OF TWO

'Do what is right for you and your family. Everyone's juggle is different.'

My childhood was idyllic. I grew up in Bunbury, two hours south of Perth in WA. Mum and Dad made a pact when they started a family that she'd stay at home and look after myself and my two younger brothers, while my dad would work. Dad had a real estate agency partnership and building company, and was involved in golf administration. We all went to the local Catholic school right through until Year 12. We would play in the sand hills that ran from our house through to the back beach in Bunbury and not come home until we were hungry.

I had two dolls but once I'd dressed them a couple of times I couldn't really understand what else you did with them. Our street was full of boys so I practised my 'death roll', went outside, got on my bike and played 'Cowboys and Indians' or 'Wars'.

CLIMBING THE CORPORATE LADDER

My first job was at Ann Waldrodt's corner store just down the road from my house. I packed the milk fridge, stocked the shelves, learned to use the meat slicer, served the customers and – my favourite – made up the bags of mixed lollies. My first pay packet was about $14 and I was beyond excited. From there I moved to Neil Lloyd's hot bread shop on Saturday mornings, where I got to take home free doughnuts and buns for our weekly barbeque. (Mum thought that was a winner.)

From an early age, my father used to joke with me to get my notebook and start taking notes because I loved listening to adult conversations at my parents' dinner parties and barbeques. I was the first in my family to get into university and excitedly moved to Perth.

I loved Perth but hated uni. I was the country kid who was just so intimidated by everything and everyone around me. My parents told me I could only drop out if I got a job. So I wrote to every newspaper, radio and television station in WA, and only one boss asked me to come in and have a chat.

A man by the name of Hartley Joynt was my ticket out of uni and into my first job as a cadet journalist at the *Wanneroo Times* in Perth, and I will be forever grateful. He hired me on the basis of a few university essays.

I started off writing the 'What's On' column about bingo nights and school fetes. I loved it and I never went back to uni. During those two years, I took voice lessons and landed a job at the Golden West Network TV station in Kalgoorlie – six hours' drive east of Perth. A bit of time in Bunbury after that, some Perth radio and then I was offered what I thought was my big city break – a reporting job at the Nine Network in Perth.

At that point I made one of the hardest decisions of my life. I turned down the Nine job to move to Los Angeles to be with my boyfriend who'd just got a job there. Turned out okay though. The boyfriend is now my husband of twenty-three years. We were together nearly six years before we even got married.

I moved to LA when I was barely twenty-two. I was scared. Moving to the east coast of Australia had never been in my grand plan for life, let alone moving to America. But I knew if I didn't follow Andrew I'd lose him, and I couldn't lose him; I loved him.

I spent several years in LA working at multiple American TV stations and covered some major news events of the time, including the fallout from the LA riots and the O.J. Simpson case.

After working all kinds of back-to-back and overnight shifts in LA, I moved back to Sydney in December 1994 and got a job straight away as a producer with Channel Seven. A few months later, Seven News hired me as a reporter. I spent the next eight years reporting for the flagship 6 p.m. nightly news bulletin and loved it. Then the executive producer of this new, fledgling Channel Seven brekky show called *Sunrise* called and needed a newsreader. My now seventeen-year-old son was eighteen months at the time, and I said yes.

EXPANDING THE FAMILY

I'd been reporting for Seven News for years and had just been given the *Late News* reading job when I fell pregnant. I started vomiting the week I found out I was pregnant and I didn't stop until the day after I delivered. I threw up all day every day and was hospitalised several times with dehydration. My pregnancies were awful. Each day was something to endure owing to the constant nausea. I put on twenty kilos each time because eating carbs seemed to help a bit. I'd eat biscuits in the ad breaks to stem the nausea then run for the bathroom after every bulletin.

'Meeting my babies was amazing in many ways.'

Meeting my babies was amazing in many ways. When I was six months pregnant with my first son, my dad died from a sudden heart attack. He was only sixty-one. So when Lachlan was born a few months later, I was still mourning Dad. I was very close to him so that day in the birthing suite was one of the most emotional of my life. Mum was there as well as Drew, my husband. It was a pretty easy birth but it was so very sad as well. The last time I saw Dad was at the twenty-week ultrasound. It was the first ultrasound he'd ever seen. He was, at first, really reluctant to come into the room, but we made him. Then he was amazed. He took that little grainy black-and-white printout of Lachlan at twenty weeks, sat it up at the bar at the Bunbury Golf Club and quoted all the stats to his mates. He was thrilled. And then he died. Just a few weeks later. I was so desperately sad. And so desperately happy that I had Lachlan. How do you deal with that?

When I had Hunter three-and-a-half years later, it was so different. We had mourned Dad and were so much more relaxed. The birth was fast and only lasted an hour. He came out blue and had to be revived so that was a bit traumatic. But we had two happy, healthy little men and we loved them more than life itself.

RETURNING TO WORK

I loved my little dudes but I really didn't enjoy staying at home, so I went back to work when each of them was about three months old. I was ready. I was doing shift work each time – *Late News* the first time around and then *Sunrise* with baby number two – so I only needed a few hours of babysitting. I missed having a purpose outside the home. I felt that work was part of my identity, part of who I was and I didn't want to stop. Even if I wasn't doing shifts, I would have done some days outside the home. I think some people are just better at staying at home with their kids and I quickly realised I wasn't one of them.

THE JUGGLE

As an organised, independent woman, I found it extremely hard to deal with the lack of sleep. Lachlan was a terrible sleeper. For eighteen months we struggled and I was very jealous of women who talked about their babies sleeping even half-way through the night. He slept for about forty-five minutes at a time and it nearly killed me. I remember being twice tested for postnatal depression and doctors telling me that because I didn't want to harm my baby, I wasn't suffering from it. Then we heard about a woman who helped people like us, Sheyne Rowley, the 'Australian Baby Whisperer.' She came to our house and taught him how to sleep in about one week. Work was my saviour in those days. It was the thing I was good at.

I refuse to feel guilty for being away from my children. When I'm at work I concentrate on doing a good job. I am lucky enough to love what I do. When I travel for work, I go wholeheartedly and don't dwell on leaving them. I have a phone full of babysitters' numbers and everywhere I go I talk to mums about who they use and get their numbers if they're willing to share. If I get the call to go away for work, sometimes within hours of a terrorist attack or a leadership spill, for example, I frantically call and call until I find somebody, or I tell the boss I can't go. I have worked at the Seven Network for twenty-four years through two pregnancies and babies, who are now seventeen and thirteen and the company has been amazingly family-friendly. If I need time off, they say run, don't walk, go and be with your sick child and we'll pick up the pieces. On the flip side, I feel like I've worked hard for them over the years too. I think it works both ways.

I've been getting up at 3 a.m. for fifteen years and my kids have had many babysitters. All our family are in WA, and my husband travels sometimes too. On those weeks we've had sitters sleep over. It's a choice we've made because our work is important to us. But let's face it, they have a great life. They are privileged children, and for their entire childhood Andrew has been there in the morning to make breakfast, school lunches and get them to school. I've picked them up, been there afterwards, made dinner and put them to bed.

The biggest struggle was probably when they were little, when just about my whole wage was going on

childcare. Not only was work important to me, but I figured that if I kept working, I'd hopefully work my way up the ladder and one day I'd earn more and need less babysitting. I was lucky that plan worked out. But for a lot of years it was really hard. Winter drags on, the kids get sick for weeks at a time, everyone is whinging, fighting and grumpy, and life is about as far away from a Kleenex commercial as you can get. I've forgotten dress-up days at school, I've forgotten to pick them up from school, I found Lachlan on a road once when he disappeared from a friend's place as a toddler. I've yelled, I've cried, I've booked them into daycare so I could just go home to a house that was silent. There were so many days that I found it so very hard being a mum. Yes, there are magical days as well. I absolutely adore my sons. They are beautiful, sensitive, caring and loving boys who I could never imagine life without. But along the way I've also had some moments where I've thought: 'I'm not very good at this. I am a bad mum, maybe I shouldn't have become one.'

MUM ADVICE

Do what's right for you and your family. Don't apologise. Don't feel guilty. Don't listen too much to other people who aren't like you. I was induced after vomiting for forty weeks because the obstetrician said, 'I think you've had enough.' I had epidurals. I only breastfed for a couple of months. I went back to work after a few months. All those things worked for me. But at times I got very stressed and upset listening to other people's opinions on these things. Everyone's juggle is different.

For the seventeen years I've had the boys, I've done shift work; first *Late News* then *Sunrise*, so I've usually needed babysitting at either end of the day. Of course, there's the last-minute stuff, like my husband's travel, my work trips, the kids' sicknesses, their school stuff . . . so that's really where the juggle kicks in. But I'm a can-do type of personality. I love being busy. I love the challenge and I get kind of excited on the days I fit it all in and get the bolognaise on the table by 6 p.m. But some days it's so hard. Don't be afraid to ask for help. I struggled on for eighteen months when Lachlan wasn't sleeping as a baby because everyone I asked (mostly other mums) told me it was normal. I was in counselling because I didn't like being a mum. I finally found a sleep expert who said, 'No, it's not normal, you need assistance,' and she helped him and us, and I learned to fall in love with him and motherhood.

HAPPINESS IS . . .

A holiday away with my family. These days everyone is so busy and everyone has a phone so it becomes very hard to have real family time unless we get ourselves out of our rut. The boys are almost adults now, so sitting around the dinner table, discussing and arguing, takes on a whole other dimension. Once upon a time it was just trying to get some protein and vegetables into their mouths, but now we're talking about drugs, sexism – all the big topics!

LESSONS FOR MY SONS

I hope to teach my sons that Mum's job is just as important as Dad's. That women can do whatever they want, just like men. And that they should show all women the same respect that they show their mum. That being part of a family is wonderful, and that not everyone is lucky enough to feel that, but that it also has to be worked at, physically and mentally, and to respect each member. Not everyone will like you in life, and you won't like everyone but that's okay. Be kind – you don't know what it's like to walk in somebody else's shoes. And . . . Mum and Dad are very lucky they found each other nearly thirty years ago and that they still love each other. If you can find that, whenever it comes along in life, hang on to it, never let it go and never, ever take it for granted.

RACHEL GILBERT

FASHION DESIGNER, MUM OF TWO

'I learn life lessons from my mother every day. She has the most incredible sense of calmness, kindness and a positive outlook on every situation.'

My childhood was spent hand in hand with my best friend in life, my sister, Vanessa. Playing dress-ups and always having her by my side in life was so comforting, fun and filled with great memories. Having two daughters of my own growing up the same age apart, has been a constant reminder of my childhood.

A PASSION FOR FASHION

I remember being fearless in my determination the day I decided to commit to creating my own brand. I knew it would be my greatest challenge and at such a young age of twenty-four, I would have to make sacrifices. Although this would seem to be a daunting moment in life, I had not one doubt that it was the right thing to do. My sheer determination and dedication drove me to work harder than I ever knew was possible.

The day I created the brand, I had put everything on the line, quit my job, taken a loan and decided to take one of the biggest risks in my career. I made a promise to myself that day: 'I would give my unwavering commitment to create a successful brand'. Over the years there are countless times when I have gone back to that promise to drive me forward.

I have been so incredibly blessed to have many 'pinch me' moments. Dressing a princess of the royal family (Princess Eugenie) was definitely one of them. Seeing my name alongside the most iconic design houses in the world in the Bergdorf Goodman elevator was another and every time I see a real bride or a customer in my creations, I have to pinch myself.

TEN YEARS OF RACHEL GILBERT

Celebrating ten years of the brand was quite overwhelming. I created a collection of ten pieces, each garment represented each year throughout the decade. It was a beautiful way to reminisce of the change and growth of the brand and I felt incredibly proud to see it all come to life in the capsule collection.

OUR FAMILY

I fell pregnant in 2013 at a time when my career was extremely fast-paced. I had just turned thirty and was travelling overseas five times a year to see clients in

'My mother has the most beautiful connection with my daughters. She teaches me to slow down when I am with them, to take time to "just be" and appreciate every moment with them.'

New York, Paris and the Middle East. 2013 also saw the opening of our second boutique, in Armadale, Victoria. It was a busy year!

I remember when they put Storm in my arms, she was screaming uncontrollably. I put my lips on her forehead to kiss her, a tear ran down my face and an immediate calm and silence came over her. She was so quiet and still, and we had our first moment of pure love. The connection was like nothing I had ever experienced in my life.

THE JUGGLE

I returned to work three months after Storm's birth and six weeks after Sloane's. The juggle has been a rollercoaster of emotions. The first few years, I really struggled. There were many tears and many conversations with my adoring mother and husband reminding me that I was doing my best. I just could not seem to make peace with dividing my time. The girls needed me, I needed the girls but my business also needed me. The brand has been such a great love for me and I have been truly blessed to have such an incredible team in my business who have given me the opportunity to be flexible to ensure I spend time with the girls.

LESSONS FROM MY MOTHER

I learn life lessons from my mother every day; my mother is my best friend.

She has the most incredible sense of calmness, kindness and a positive outlook on every situation. My mother has the most beautiful connection with my daughters. She teaches me to slow down when I am with them, to take time to 'just be' and appreciate every moment with them. My mother has also taught me to drop everything and take advantage of those moments with the girls, such as sitting on the floor with them playing hairdressers or doing a puzzle. These are the moment I really connect with the girls and the moments I cherish the most.

Today, I have a different perspective of things and have structured my life to be extremely organised to ensure I make time for all aspects of my life. Don't get me wrong, balls drop every now and again. As I am writing this in the office this morning, my husband called as we had both forgotten our carer is off today and he will be dropping Sloane into my work today. It is all a work in progress.

LESSONS FOR MY DAUGHTERS

Lessons for my daughters are to be yourself and not to be influenced by others. To be grateful every single day.

HAPPINESS IS . . .

Any time my girls, Tom and I are laughing together.

MY MOTTO IS . . .

Be grateful for what you have, be disciplined and determined to get what you want to achieve, and remember to stop and enjoy those precious moments with your family.

Natural
pure pops

CANDICE LAKE

PHOTOGRAPHER, BLOGGER, CONTRIBUTING STYLE EDITOR AT *VOGUE*, MUM

'Meeting my two babies was an extension of how they were in the womb. The fierce and overwhelming love is something I just didn't know I was capable of.'

I spent my childhood in rural Brisbane. It was such an idyllic upbringing in the country. Our home was on stilts in a gorgeous valley and a creek wrapped around it. My siblings and I would spend all day along the creek exploring for miles, getting lost in the bush and climbing trees. My mother would call out to us for mealtimes, but other than that we were completely free. I remember being quite frustrated once I became a teenager about how remote we were, although it made me get quite creative and I ended up hosting camping and full-moon parties in the yard. Once I ran away on the ride-on mower . . . I obviously didn't get very far! I long for my children to have a similar upbringing, so deeply connected to nature.

CAREER CLIMB

I think modelling was an amazing vehicle to drive me towards photography. I had always wanted to go to art school when I was younger, although somehow I ended up at law school. A couple of years into it, I luckily fell into modelling and everything else went out the window. I met the most extraordinary people and experienced things I never would have had access to without modelling. It was an accelerated life lesson and

it was a few years later while between shots on a shoot for *Harper's Bazaar,* when I asked the photographer if I could possibly come with him on his next shoot to assist. That was how I began assisting fashion photographers and transitioned to the other side of the camera, while gaining a Bachelor of Fine Arts degree. Without modelling I would never have had these amazing opportunities in photography.

CAREER HIGHLIGHTS

My career highlights include seeing my first Ralph Lauren and Versace campaigns when I was starting out. Working with Alberta Ferretti to make my wedding dress, being an active part of the creative process and seeing it

'Speak to your children like they are the wisest, kindest, most beautiful and magical humans on earth. For what they believe, they will become.'

covered in *Vogue US*. This was a very personal journey full of emotions. Becoming the face and global ambassador of TRESemmé was an amazing experience. *Vogue US* doing a feature on me in their best dressed issue. Having my university graduating exhibition covered in *Vogue* magazine. Having my first exhibition in New York. Travelling to Shanghai with Louis Vuitton to photograph a story for *Vogue* – an incredibly exciting and eye opening experience that began an ongoing relationship shooting for the brand. Shooting campaigns for Cartier and Jimmy Choo. And finally, having a fashion label, Candidate, with General Pants Co. for six years.

THE JUGGLE

My career was at its height, with me travelling about nine months out of the year, right up until I was about to pop with both my children! I didn't look as pregnant as I was, so I got away with a lot more than I should have. I don't think I fully grasped the intensity of how having a baby would change our lives and I just kept going. I was shooting a campaign for Jo Malone on location in London four days before Olympia arrived. Retrospectively, I see photos of myself and wonder what the hell I was doing! I regret not taking even just a week off before they came to just rest and recharge.

MEETING MY BABIES

I will never forget the moments when my children were born. I was so lucky to feel immediately connected to them upon finding out their sex. It is funny how much you can tell about their personality from how they are in the womb. Arden was so chilled that I was forever getting him checked at hospital – he always had his legs crossed and arms behind his head – chilling. Olympia was a complete force of nature and didn't stop moving all day and all night. Their personalities now exactly match their temperament in the womb. Meeting them was just an extension of this. The fierce and overwhelming love I feel for them is something I just didn't know I was capable of. 'Where is this free-flowing, never-ending river of love coming from?' I would often ask myself.

THE CHALLENGES

I think because I am such a control freak in the rest of my life, I was very much taken aback when I had to be induced rather suddenly during labour, due to a severe intrahepatic cholestasis. I had planned a home birth with Arden, with my doula and midwife, and had an 800-litre pool set up in my sitting room, ready to go! I was rushed to the hospital (for both births) and told I would certainly not be having the kind of labour I had planned. It was all quite intense and stressful, and I wish I had been open to looking at alternative birthing options beforehand as I was quite overwhelmed with the changes.

I had also that imagined breastfeeding would be the most natural experience in the world, but my son had such difficulty. After eight weeks of trying literally everything under the sun and him rapidly losing weight, I exclusively pumped until he was one – which was the hardest thing I have done in my entire life. I would set my alarm every three hours and pump for forty minutes, then feed him and get an hour of sleep before doing it all again. All day and all night.

Olympia fed incredibly well, although I was travelling a lot for work when she was small, so I would pump all through the night for weeks before I left on a trip to ensure she had enough milk. I also, of course, had to pump while away – I've pumped on buses in India, on a seaplane to the Maldives, in dodgy loos, hotel rooms, the Eurostar – the glamour of it all. I have no idea how I managed to do this, although I think retrospectively it was the guilt of not being able to take maternity leave which I found so challenging, so I decided I would do whatever it took to nourish my children 100 per cent with my milk.

THE PRESSURES

There is a huge amount of pressure on women to continue with their career, while growing and then nourishing a

baby. We are expected to 'bounce back' physically, thrive in a work environment, bake cookies for school bake sales and still maintain healthy relationships with our partners and friends. It's a hell of a lot to deal with while hormonally imbalanced and seriously sleep deprived. It was a great gift to be able to breastfeed and pump for my children, because I had the wonderful support of my husband and the financial means to employ a nanny while I worked. So many women have no support and that is something we need to address. The biggest change is the sleep deprivation. I think I worked out that I lost 900 hours of sleep in the first year of Arden's life. Learning to function on little sleep was incredibly intense.

RETURNING TO WORK

I started back at work four weeks after having my first child, Arden. I was contractually bound to Unilever with a haircare brand and I had to fly to New York for two weeks to shoot and film. This was an incredibly difficult time as I was still struggling to breastfeed. I had had a very difficult birth experience (vastly different to how I had planned), so I was trying to deal with all of this – while keeping up the facade professionally that I was still exactly the same person I had been pre-baby.

I will never forget an email I received from a client three days after my son was born. 'Congratulations on the birth of your baby boy! We'd love to shoot you for our campaign in New York next week – would you be able to pop over for a few days?' This pretty much sums up how the fashion industry treats motherhood. Hide it until you absolutely cannot, then bounce back within a matter of weeks and hand your baby over to someone else to raise. I found having a baby very conflicting both professionally and personally. Having children and wanting to really stop and enjoy the precious and limited time with them in the middle of building a brand was incredibly challenging. It felt impossible to balance the two. I travelled everywhere with my son so we were never separated in the first year, and I only took on jobs that were really important to me. It ended up being a really positive experience and made me assess my professional direction, although it was quite difficult at the time.

With Olympia I was not as lucky as I was with Arden, as I was travelling to incredibly remote places on jobs that I was contractually bound to over long periods of time, and thus I could not take her. It was difficult to be away from her and I am sure a major factor in my choice to why I breastfeed her for almost two years.

SECRETS TO THE JUGGLE

Having help has been key. For the first year of Arden's life, I tried to do everything by myself with no help from any family and I found I was constantly conflicted. I was still working and travelling with my son, while being a full-time mum, and it was overwhelming. Now, my main aim is that whatever I am putting my energy into, I am giving it 100 per cent. We now have a wonderful nanny so that I can focus 100 per cent on my career during the day and then when I am with my children in the morning and afternoon, I give them my full and undivided attention. I realised after that first year of trying to do it all that it really is about quality and not quantity of time. Once I accepted this, our life was a lot richer.

I also think transcendental mediation has been really key in keeping the balance in my life. Just taking twenty–thirty minutes a day for myself has done wonders – but I need to do more of this! When I practise I am noticeably a lot calmer and I am clearer. It is essentially like downloading all the noise and taking a long breath.

I am also so lucky that my husband fully took on the role of equal parent. Without him, I would not be able to do anything and the juggle wouldn't exist.

I was very lucky and lost the baby weight almost immediately after birth, but I am sure it is a body type thing. Although, with both my babies I had quite a bit of trouble breastfeeding so I intentionally gained about seven kilograms postpartum each time, as they say you need the extra weight for milk supply. So I did it all in reverse. I think the most incredible thing I have heard is 'nine months in and nine months out'. It basically means it took your body nine months to create a baby and you shouldn't even think about losing any body weight for at least nine months after giving birth. Pregnancy has become quite transactional – and we tend to forget the intensity it has on women's bodies.

HEALTH AND WELLBEING

I don't devote enough time to this – AT ALL! It is on the top of my to-do list. I am blessed and cursed with my body. I am so incredibly lucky to be quite thin naturally, so I have never had to do any exercise to stay in shape. However as I get older, I am really feeling the pull to get strong and stay healthy. I did try a trainer recently although I found the entire experience quite counter-intuitive and aggressive. I have always loved swimming but after you've swum morning laps in an ocean pool, the local pool in London doesn't cut it! Olivia Palermo put me onto her trainer, who has been known to get incredible results, although again, I just didn't feel it. I like really calming exercise.

I am, however, incredibly healthy at home and we eat really well. My husband and I made a conscious decision to not give our kids sugar and ensure they are really nourished with everything they eat. We buy locally and organically. It is a very privileged thing to be able to invest in and we are very aware of that, although we feel it is so important that our kids know that carrots grow in the ground and for them to actually grow them and watch the entire process. Also, we wanted to take them to restaurants that we loved. They eat everything from Indian dhal to lentil pies and fresh fish with ginger. We make a conscious effort to all eat the same food and all together. That way no one is substituting anything and we all eat really well. Basically, the kids are beyond excited to have a medjool date or cashew butter on a rice cracker as a treat.

LESSONS FROM MY MOTHER

My mother taught me so many things, but especially resilience – if you want something, go fight for it. Never take no for an answer. You may be rejected thirty times before someone gives you a shot, but someone will always give you a shot. If you want something badly enough, you can always get it.

My mother lost both her parents when she was a teenager and then had three children by the time she was twenty-six. With three small children at home and no financial or emotional support from external family, she somehow managed to build an incredibly successful career as a businesswoman in an all-male industry. She is a force and such an inspiration. I definitely get my incessant determination and self-belief from my mother.

Love your children for who they are and not who you envisage them to be. I love the quote: 'Speak to your children as if they are the wisest, kindest, most beautiful and magical humans on the earth. For what they believe is what they will become.'

HAPPINESS IS . . .

Anywhere with the kids, preferably by the sea.

THREE THINGS THAT MAKE ME SMILE . . .

The four of us dancing at 6 a.m. in our pyjamas, swimming in the sea just a little too far out in the scorching hot sun and sneaking in for cuddles while they are asleep.

MY ROLE MODEL IS . . .

Women who seemingly juggle perfectly. Angela Ahrendts, Senior Vice President of Apple Retail, is top of my list. She transformed Burberry into a $13 billion business and is now doing great things over at Apple . . . and she has three children.

MOTTO

My motto has always been: 'You must do what you're afraid to do. If something seems easy, you're not pushing yourself hard enough.' To create something out of nothing is incredibly difficult. When people say to me, 'Your job is amazing,' I don't think they realise the insane amount of work that goes into it. Being your own brand is the most empowering thing, but it is also an incredible amount of work. As Ralph Waldo Emerson said: 'The only person you are destined to become is the person you decide to be.'

PIP EDWARDS

FOUNDER OF P.E NATION, MOTHER TO JUSTICE

'I can't quite pinpoint it exactly, but I have a dedication to succeed, to succeed for my son, for my family, but not materialistically, more for that tangible achievement in leaving a mark and legacy.'

Growing up, I fondly remember hanging in the street with all my neighbours. I lived in a beautiful cul-de-sac on the North Shore, and all the kids in the street used to ride bikes and play outside for hours. I loved that freedom and exploration. I also spent a lot of my childhood playing the piano. Many, many hours were spent on those ivory keys, practising like crazy. The piano was an incredible inspiration, as music is a major part of who I am and how I explore emotion, which has invoked a lot of passion in my life.

PASSION FOR FASHION

My career actually started out in the corporate world when I was twenty-one, at PricewaterhouseCoopers. I worked in global risk management for nearly three years before I did a complete one-eighty and uprooted myself from the corporate career path to work in fashion.

I started working in PR at Ksubi in 2004, and then later, moved into the design team where I focused on women's wear. In 2009, I moved to sass & bide as senior creative and accessories designer, with a focus on collection creative briefs. In 2013 I jumped ship from the designer to mass market, to operate as design director for retail giant General Pants Co., not only focusing on the right product offering by demographic, but working very closely with the marketing team across all channels and retail operations. It was then in 2016, while I was still working at General Pants, that I launched P.E Nation.

Two years later, P.E Nation boasts over 200 stockists across 150 countries, with a very strong online presence. I am super proud of my little love child that I share with my business partner and best friend, Claire Tregoning.

I definitely didn't realise that having my own brand was my calling, however, my career trajectory, working knowledge and experience armed me with the right tools to be equipped to actually do it. It really came down to the concept. And it was the concept that inspired me. I took the idea to Claire and together we were lucky enough to both have had the working history, with some idea of a road map on how to roll out a brand and set up the structure, and bring in the right the people and processes to build this from the ground up. Having worked for three huge and very different businesses set me up for the task and made my dream concept actually doable.

BECOMING A MOTHER

I was working at Ksubi with the father of my child at the

adidas

time I fell pregnant. It was very much an extended family at Ksubi; we were all dear friends, living a lifestyle that created the Ksubi movement. I have to admit, I didn't take to being a mother that easily. I had actually never really held a baby until Justice was born! I had just turned twenty-six and was definitely one of the first in my group of friends to become a mother. The unknown was daunting and the responsibility was overwhelming as I felt like I was still a child myself! But his big, blue eyes and gorgeous lips and skin, which he still has today (Justice is now twelve), just made my heart complete. I knew he was my everything. Justice would be the reason why I did anything and everything. He would become my driving force. It was going to be 'just us'.

Being a mother is such an amazing experience. Justice is his own person with a vibrant, sensitive and funny character. I just can't believe that this awesome little human is mine. I'm super lucky to be his mum. And I'm super lucky that we have grown up together in a way.

THE JUGGLE

After having Justice, the challenges included juggling the craziness of my life at the time, being part of the whirlwind that was Ksubi, with a partner who travelled a lot for work and for me to have to sacrifice that life to fulfil my motherly role. It was a real shift in my way of life; a shift that was the greatest thing that could have ever happened to me. I was so young and had to learn so much, but I was going to learn it all with my child by my side. There was so much trial and error, so much emotion and, at times, it felt impossible. My baby daddy and I separated when Justice was two years old and I found myself really reliant on my parents to assist me in raising my son, so that he would not be affected.

Of course, my life has completely changed. Justice is number one. And my work is also a top priority, in order to provide for him and give him the opportunities I want him to have. He is my ultimate person, my best friend, my room mate, my confidant, the reason and purpose for everything that I do. Without him, I would be lost. He keeps me balanced and real and selfless and absolutely challenges me at times, for the better. He makes me think twice and question life and what it's all about, which is so important when I work day in, day out, in a crazy and sometimes superficial industry where meaning can be consumed by vanity. He is the visual timeline of my life – I can see how far we have come, how far I have come and how much more we have to do, together! Despite it being exhausting and taxing at times, I would not do life without him.

RETURNING TO WORK

I went back to work after two months as I'm a worker, but I also needed that stimulation. Being new to motherhood and its demands was confronting and work almost came as a relief. I had amazing parents to lean on and ask for help, and I felt more like myself being back at work. Now in hindsight, I wish I had taken more time in those early years to really understand that early learning phase.

Ksubi was at its prime, demanding and globally flying, and I was young and wanted the best of both worlds. But, as we all know, that's impossible. The only way to juggle it all was with the incredible assistance of my parents, who took Justice on like their own. I'm an only child, so it was as if they had a chance to be involved with raising another child, and one that was a boy. As a single mother the juggle was real, the guilt was real, the missing-out-on-some-firsts was real, but I had to work full-time to pay the bills, so there was no choice. Survival was the reality. My journey of motherhood definitely had a rocky start, but wow, did I grow and learn my way through to now truly understand what life's about and how incredible my commitment to my son really is.

CREATING P.E NATION

Launching P.E Nation in 2016 has definitely been my major career highlight. Within the business there have been so many amazing moments; our debut Mercedes-Benz Fashion Week Australia show two months after we launched, two sell-out collaborations with Reebok, a pop-up store in Selfridges, London, being honoured with numerous prestigious awards and the launch of our menswear at MBFWA this year are some of the standouts.

Creating the brand has been a very organic process for Claire and I, which I love. I think that's how things have to roll. We have an amazing work history and share the same eyes and ears. A lot of that comes into play when you're starting a new business, but we've fast-tracked past that. We have the same gut feeling about things so it's great to be on the same page. P.E is really an extension of Claire and me; fashion-focused activewear for women just like us – busy, working mothers who are

'Being a mother is such an amazing experience. He is his own person with a vibrant, sensitive and funny character. I just can't believe that this awesome little human is mine.'

interested in fashion and sport, and like to keep fit!

BRAND SUCCESS

P.E Nation is definitely no overnight success. Claire and I have been in the industry, essentially doing this 'forever'. P.E comes from a place of passion, experience and working knowledge, with a very well-thought-out strategy and structure for major scale. Knowledge and experience is the power. Also, a strong sense of self goes a really long way. And both of these come with age.

We have merged great product with strong visual identity, along with a lifestyle attached to the brand, so that is what people are buying into – our vision, vibe and the community that we have created.

The brand has been worn by celebrities around the world, and featured many times on the television show *Keeping Up With the Kardashians*. Kylie Jenner and her sisters Khloé and Kourtney Kardashian have all sported P.E Nation, even taking to their influential Instagram and Snapchat feeds to spruik the brand.

We still high five when we see the Kardashians wearing the brand. They're such a powerful family.

Personally, the work ethic instilled by my parents has been a major player in my success. Early on, I was taught to earn my keep. This diligence and dedication to work has always stuck. My career has been purely inspired by following what I love and being a sponge to everything about the fashion industry. I am responsible for inspiring my career. I can't quite pinpoint it exactly, but I have a dedication to succeed; to succeed for my son, for my family, but not materialistically, more for that tangible achievement of leaving a mark and legacy. I'm not here to be another statistic or number, I feel I'm more than that.

HEALTH AND WELLBEING

My approach is probably what most people say, and that is one of balance. I love super-clean eating, I love my exercise and having a routine, I love seeing different specialists for advice and I love my own version of what mindfulness is to me. However, I also love to go out, drink, dance and let go a little! That's the balance.

MY ROLE MODELS

I have many. My mother for her dedication, my partner for his encouragement and belief in me, and my close friends for their undying support. Through my work I have been fortunate enough to meet so many awesome, unreal and inspiring people who have really raised the bar. They have raised the bar in fashion, in being creatives, in business and in sport ... and all these people are role models to me. I am so lucky that I surround myself with the best people, and together we keep raising that bar!

SUCCESS IS . . .

Loving what you do for a living, and loving doing that job every single day. And if you get to create the opportunity of starting your own business, the privilege is all mine and I should be so lucky that I get to call the shots and present a business that reflects me and my ethos and culture and passion and love . . . I've actually hit success in its true sense. Success is this feeling.

HAPPINESS IS . . .

Happiness is being free and vulnerable, yet confident to be your true self.

THREE THINGS THAT MAKE ME SMILE

Justice, the sun and the snow.

ANTIHERO

KATHRYN EISMAN

JOURNALIST, DESIGNER, BESTSELLING AUTHOR, MUM OF TWO

'Meeting my babies for the first time was a feeling of deep, soul-opening gratitude. I wasn't prepared for the immense love I felt as they looked into my eyes for the first time.'

I remember the simplicity of my childhood. I think I spent every single day of my summer holidays on the beach just covered in sand and salt water. I'd go for swims at Bondi Beach before school with my dad, regardless of whether it was sunny or in the midst of a thunderstorm. I was obsessed with running and would train after school most days. At home, I remember spending a lot of time in my room writing poetry, often deeply depressing poetry, and often three to four poems a day. My parents were really worried at one point, but I kept reminding them that apparently some of the most uplifting classical music was written when the composer was in the midst of a deep depression, so the opposite was true for me!

Looking back, I'm grateful to have found such a healthy outlet for the heightened emotions of my youth. I remember our family holidays most clearly, be it going to the Blue Mountains with my brother and sister, hiking twelve-hour bushwalks, or flying to Italy or America and doing epic month-long holidays. From my own childhood, I've learned that it's in the 'downtime', the in-between scheduled activities, that creativity and dreams grow.

MY CAREER

I was the youngest person in my grade at high school and graduated shortly after I turned seventeen. Days later, I walked into a modelling agency with a photo that a photographer had taken of me playing water polo at Club Med in a crochet bikini. They sent me out on a casting that day and told me to tell the client that my book was being 'updated'. I booked the job and the next four, and was signed immediately. The world really opened up to me through modelling, and I got to meet so many creative and interesting people, and to venture out of the eastern suburbs of Sydney. Around that time, by coincidence, the then editor of *Vogue*, Marion Hume, moved in next door to where I lived. She saw something in me that I didn't see in myself and really encouraged me to venture into the world of fashion. Even then, I remember admiring her career and being far more interested in writing about fashion than just modelling it. While I was modelling I started writing my first book, *How to Tell a Man by His Shoes*, born from my fascination with the connection between what we wear and who we are. By the time I had graduated from university (aged twenty-one), having studied Communications Journalism at UTS, the book had been published in ten countries and become an international bestseller. Shortly after, I moved to New York on a book tour.

MY INSPIRATION

Fashion is often accused of being superficial, but why someone decides to wear a particular item of clothing and to literally walk through life with it as an extension of themselves is deeply revealing. I always knew that we reveal ourselves in the details not the grand declarations; the little things we do when we don't think anyone is noticing. No one had ever written about the link between who we are and what we wear. I sent the manuscript of my first book to three publishers, honestly expecting nothing would come of it. Within a week, I had a bidding war between two of them, ultimately signing a six-figure three-book publishing deal. My second book, *How to Tell a Woman by Her Handbag,* then delved into our true purse-onality.

NEW YORK, NEW YORK

That old Charles Dickens quote, 'It was the best of times, it was the worst of times,' is pretty accurate when describing my move to New York. It was the making of me. I left behind any comfort and stability, and moved there at the age of twenty-one with a small suitcase of summer clothes, not knowing a soul, in the dead of winter. After spending a few months moving from apartment to apartment in the snow and sleeping on sofas, I rented an illegal structure on the rooftop of a once-grand but now dilapidated townhouse on the best street in Manhattan. It was so cold during the winter that the pipes would freeze. Within three months I was contracted to be the youngest on-air reporter for NBC in New York, interviewing everyone from President Clinton to covering New York Fashion Week. It was like being given the key to the city. There were many lonely times and I remember having to grow a thick skin pretty quickly in order to survive, but it was a defining moment in my life and has made me who I am today.

LOOKING BACK . . .

There have been countless amazing, surreal experiences, like emceeing the fundraiser for the then Mayor of New York, Rudi Giuliani, interviewing President Clinton backstage at Radio City Music Hall, receiving two Emmy Award nominations for my work at *E! News* in LA, walking the red carpet at the Academy Awards, or just seeing my little book in print in the biggest bookstores around the world and winning *Cosmopolitan* magazine's Fun Fearless Female Author of the Year! But the truth is, media isn't a linear path, so I'm as grateful today for every opportunity to do what I love as I was when I first started out.

EXPANDING THE FAMILY

I was living in Los Angeles with my husband, Siimon Reynolds, when I was offered the position of Head of Fashion and Lifestyle at *E! News*. I was eight months pregnant at the time. It was the dream job and the show that had inspired me to move to LA in the first place, so I felt I would regret it if I didn't accept. They kindly waited until I'd had the baby then called me to ask if I still wanted the job and asked how much time off I'd like. I asked for three months. Six-and-a-half weeks later I was running coverage there. It was a time of tremendous growth, learning to be a mother for the first time while fulfilling a very demanding new role.

Before you have kids it's easy to give all of yourself to your work. It's exhilarating being 'all in'; the late nights at the office, the single-minded focus. When I became a mum, my priorities immediately shifted. I didn't want to miss a thing when it came to my kid, but I also didn't want to lose myself. I wanted to get my work done to perfection and then get home as soon as I could to be with my child. There were many times at *E!* when I would not go to the bathroom because I was pushing myself to get so much done and I didn't want to lose time urinating! Ha!
I was forced to find ways to do an excellent job and give 100 per cent of myself, but with only 50 per cent of the time. I think every working mother wishes she could have another six hours per day. I love work and feel privileged

to do what I do, but I know that nothing is more important than my children and the transient magic of having a young family and little people who, for now, want nothing more than to spend time with their mama.

MEETING MY DAUGHTERS

It was a feeling of deep, soul-opening gratitude! When they handed me my babies and I saw they were both healthy, I felt like I'd won the lottery. I wasn't prepared for the immense love I felt as they looked into my eyes for the first time. Knowing that I am literally their life source, their protector. It makes me want to be the best version of myself for them. When they sent me home with Capri, I was like, 'Are you sure you want to do that?' I was so green!

THE CHALLENGES

No one gives you a manual for parenthood, so you often just hope you're doing a good job. I've definitely been forced to be much more organised and really plan my day. I rarely feel like I've mastered the juggle, but I keep showing up to the circus and I think maybe that's the most important thing.

HIGH HEEL JUNGLE

In a sea of glossy fashion, food and family blogs, I wanted to create an online space that spoke to all the varied aspects of a woman's life and saw her as a whole, not just a 'mummy' or a 'fashionista' or a 'career woman', but all of the above and so much more! I have always believed that a woman needn't sacrifice her style for substance, or her family for career success, but I do know first-hand how hard the juggling act can be. I created highheeljungle.com to share everything I've learned while doing my own juggling act. There are articles on how to ask for a pay rise, having a younger boss, a very personal letter about motherhood, the psychology of fashion, and then, of course, there's a lot of honest, raw celebrity interviews with everyone from Reese Witherspoon to Kerry Washington!

EXPANDING THE BRAND

I couldn't find a pair of socks that felt really luxurious and fun, and that instantly gave my outfit that 'fashion' point of view, so I created High Heel Jungle socks! I'd wear them while interviewing celebrities for my TV show and almost everyone from Lucy Hale to Isla Fisher to Lupita Nyong'o stopped the interview to ask about them and wanted a pair, sometimes even taking my pair off me! We got picked up Fred Segal in the US and the business has grown month by month since launch. I wanted to launch the socks as a celebration of women by creating a product that was at once luxurious and transformative, that could take a woman's outfit and her mood from here to there with the simple addition of an accessory, and without breaking the bank or having to invest a huge amount of money like other statement accessories. I've tried to be as fearless in the way I've launched the line as in the spirit of the collection itself. If you have an idea, a passion or a calling, we need to go for it, to back ourselves, to figure it out as we do it instead of pondering the 'what-ifs' on the sideline. No one has all the answers, but the only way to figure things out is by actually diving in headfirst. My hope is that these socks become your best friend, something you can turn to each day and say: 'Hmmm . . . who do I feel like being today? Am I feeling romantic in our Crystal Lace sheer socks, am I feeling sexy in our Catch 'Em Fishnet socks, am I feeling cosy in our Velvet Galaxy socks, or am I feeling like I need our Leave Me Alone socks?' You get to wear your heart on your socks, instead of your sleeve!

I have also created something called Trifecta

'When I became a mum, my priorities immediately shifted. I didn't want to miss a thing when it came to my kids but I also didnt want to lose myself.'

'I think every working mother wishes she could have another six hours per day.'

Coaching to help women reach the highest level possible in each category.

THE JUGGLE

I launched High Heel Jungle socks weeks before I gave birth. I felt like I was bringing two babies into the world. I've found motherhood the greatest source of inspiration – I want to put beautiful, meaningful things into the world. I want my daughters to grow up seeing a mother fulfilled in every sense and know that they can have the same for themselves.

SOCIAL MEDIA

I think it's created a society of comparison. People viewing the false highlights reel of someone else's life and thinking they don't measure up. I read somewhere that comparison is the thief of happiness and I think it's so true. That's why I call it Insta-sham, because it's not a real depiction of anyone's life and we need to remember that. What I do like is the democratisation of media; people can now use social media to build a personal brand and platform that was simply impossible before and monopolised by the major media companies. This platform allows many women to redefine work, even working from home, so they can spend more time with their families. I like that aspect very much.

MY APPROACH TO HEALTH AND WELLBEING IS . . .

Pilates mixed with chocolate.

THREE THINGS THAT MAKE ME SMILE . . .

My family (Capri, Monet and Siimon), my brother and sister, my mum and dad. I am obsessed with family.

MY ROLE MODEL IS . . .

My grandmother Anna Reich (the namesake for Monet's middle name). She was the epitome of what it is to be a lady, extremely well spoken, a formidable businesswoman, extremely beautiful and stylish, philanthropic, and a survivor of the Holocaust who never let it define her and remained eternally optimistic.

Above all, she valued family and kindness.

HAPPINESS IS . . .

Working hard and laughing even harder with family and friends. In my experience, women feel happy when these three aspects of their life are at a high point: 1. Career or contribution 2. Health and beauty. 3. Relationships.

ICE CREAM

YOU ARE NOT JUST RAISING YOUR SON, YOU ARE RAISING SOMEBODY'S HUSBAND, SOMEBODY'S FATHER: RAISE HIM WELL.

Photo credit: Bianca Cheah

ELLE HALLIWELL

AUTHOR, COLUMNIST, MUM

'My childhood was fairly idyllic. I was very fortunate to grow up by the water, and spent most of my days fishing off our jetty, looking for mud crabs, making cubby houses and being dressed up like a doll by my two much older sisters.'

I always wanted to travel the world and, from a young age, had a flair for writing and photography. I initially wanted to be a photographer and a journalist, but quickly found out that you had to choose one if you wanted to be taken seriously. Nowadays it's pretty common to do both, thanks to the rise of social media, but back then it was unheard of, so I chose writing.

BECOMING A MUM

Before we decided to have a baby, I was fashion editor at *The Daily Telegraph*. My role involved covering fashion and celebrity stories as well as attending events a few times per week. I was also studying nutrition, working at Nova 96.9 and reporting on showbiz news on Channel Nine. It was a very hectic time. At the beginning of my pregnancy, I was diagnosed with blood cancer (chronic myeloid leukaemia). So I was figuratively holding my breath for eight months, hoping things would turn out okay. I didn't really think too much about what would come next, so seeing my son for the first time was a complete mix of shock, love and trepidation.

The biggest challenge was trying to manage my illness but also enjoy the pregnancy as a first-time mum. It was a very confusing and emotional period, so looking after myself, and my mental and physical health, was a constant challenge.

LIFE CHANGES

I'm not the person I used to be. Cancer and motherhood forced me to look at who I was up until that point and figure out what I would and would no longer accept when it came to my life. I became much more aligned to my values, and with that came a softening of my personality. I like to think that I returned to a more authentic, vulnerable version of myself, which I felt I had lost somewhat during my decade working in media and showbiz. Life is a little rawer and perhaps harder in a

'I felt as though I had been given another chance at life, and there were things I wanted to share with the world that I simply couldn't do as a stay-at-home mum.'

Photo credit: Bianca Cheah

Photo credit: Bianca Cheah

sense, but I've found a beauty in that. I now try to make decisions and speak from my heart, rather than my ego.

GOING BACK TO WORK

I always believed that if I had the choice financially, I would stay at home until my children began primary school, but I realised fairly soon after becoming a mum that I wasn't destined for this. I felt as though I had been given another chance at life, and there were things I wanted to share with the world that I simply couldn't do as a stay-at-home mum. It's a constant emotional tug of war, but I'm starting to find more balance and try to give my son my complete attention when I'm with him, and my work my complete attention when I'm there. Being half-present as a mum and an employee just causes unnecessary stress and guilt.

THE JUGGLE

The balls regularly drop, and I find it hard to say no to opportunities which come my way, but I know how important it is to look after myself in order to be strong enough to care for my son. I'm fortunate enough to have a hands-on husband and amazing in-laws who care for my son weekly, and most of the time we make it work, but it's not easy. I do struggle with guilt that I can't be with him more, especially now that he can verbalise his displeasure at me leaving for work (which kills me!).

FAMILY TIME

I try to rest on weekends, so they are usually very low key, spent with our families and close friends. We usually start our weekends at our local farmers markets in Bondi Beach, buying groceries for the week and visiting the chai tent. The markets are at the local primary school, so Tor always looks forward to a session on the play equipment.

HEALTHY LIVING

I'm studying naturopathy and health coaching right now, so my approach to and understanding of nutrition and health is constantly evolving. I'm very conscious of what I put in and on my body, as well as my son's, but I like to stick to journalist Michael Pollan's philosophy when it comes to my diet, which is: 'Eat food, mostly plants, not too much.' I think we've taken the common sense out of eating, and made what is such a primal, intuitive process much too complicated. I'm currently still being treated for my cancer, and it has taken its toll on my body and immune system, so I also see a naturopath regularly to try and negate the effects of the drugs.

THE CHALLENGES

I think any form of rejection is one of the hardest aspects of a professional career. Being told you're not good enough, not right for a role or simply being dumped from a position without a good explanation as to why can be a real hit to your ego. But every time it happens it gets a little easier, and it's so common in the media industry. It's also quite challenging staying relevant in a fast-paced industry, so I've found it really beneficial to upskill and keep learning. Success to me is feeling you have found, and are living your purpose. My biggest career highlight has been adding 'author' to my resume when I launched my memoir, *A Mother's Choice*.

THINGS THAT MAKE ME SMILE . . .

Cats, my family and witnessing acts of kindness.

BEST ADVICE I'VE BEEN GIVEN AS A MOTHER

Don't google it!

HAPPINESS IS . . .

Being alive!

NIKKI PHILLIPS

MEDIA PERSONALITY, FASHION BLOGGER, MOTHER TO JETT

'I struggled at first juggling having a baby and a career, and endured much anxiety. It was a big change.'

I had the most incredible childhood. I grew up in New Zealand and my memories are of always being outdoors. We had a holiday house on Lake Taupo, so I remember always being active, happy and carefree. I also grew up horse riding, surrounded by animals and being fortunate enough to travel to magical places as a child. My parents really did shower us with incredible adventures.

MEETING JETT

This is a moment no one can prepare you for. I felt utter contentment. I was overwhelmed yet bursting with love. We had struggled for years, so to actually hold our son after all we had endured was the best feeling in the world. Safe to say I don't think I blinked for five days. My eyes were wide open, staring and in awe of what we had created. The biggest challenge so far has been the lack of independence. All of a sudden this was taken away from me. My body was always needed to care for this little man. Simple chores and work opportunities became increasingly hard to tackle. Learning to initially juggle mum life with work was something I struggled with, as I never thought I would be able to go back to the way things were and it all seemed too overwhelming. Let me count the ways life has changed since having a baby: no sleep, no alone time, anxiety about whether or not I'm a good parent … did I mention no sleep? But I love it. I've become much more patient and aware of all the small things. He has put everything into perspective for me. Life is more fulfilling.

THE JUGGLE

I struggled at first juggling having a baby and a career, and endured much anxiety. It was a big change and we have no family in Sydney, where we choose to live. I think firstly I had to come to terms with the fact that this is my life now, a constant struggle is always going to exist. I just need to learn to manage it as best I can. Find a balance that works for me and, most importantly, Jett. We have two staffies, so we love getting out with them to the local

'When it comes to happiness, my nearest and dearest really matter the most.'

LA

park or beach. We love going on picnics and family date nights to local restaurants.

My routine can only be described as chaotic! I try to maintain a similar routine to the one I had prior to being a mother. Such as continuing training sessions three days per week, working from home four hours a day, doing blog shoots twice a week. However, sometimes I realise those things just aren't going to happen due to now having to be aware of sleep routines (which vary), sporadic mood swings, milestones and sicknesses. I think trying to keep a routine is key, but realising that some days it doesn't go to plan and that's okay. This is just us and we are doing the best we can.

I know it's a cliché but I would have to say my proudest achievement is Jett. What my body was capable of in creating this perfect specimen, and just now doing life with him is by far the best thing I ever did in life!

THE CLIMB

I was very young when I started modelling, and fell into it unexpectedly. I always admired women with immense work ethic and drive so I guess over the years there have been many women who have inspired me and I'm constantly inspired on a regular basis by colleagues and women within my industry.

I think every job has its challenges. Mine is no different. But one thing that really upsets me within my industry is the open body shaming and negativity that goes with being in the public eye. Body shaming is something I struggled with when I was young, before I became smart enough to feel more sorry for the people doing the attacking than for myself. Being confident no matter what your size, looks or physique, is the strongest tool that sometimes causes more jealously within others. Be the best version of you!

So many people think success is about building wealth, having the perfect everything, launching a billion-dollar business or having a large social media following! To me, success is knowing that I did my best; my best at work no matter how small or big the job. Showing respect to all and always being the best version of me. Keeping family close and always being positive and happy. That to me is success. All the rest doesn't matter.

HEALTHY LIVING

I've always been a very active person. I love exercise and being outdoors. I've never watched what I eat, but I am by nature a healthy eater and I love naughty foods too, but in moderation. I think for me the best way to approach health and wellbeing is naturally and not forced.

LESSONS FROM MY MOTHER

My mother is one in a million. She is the kindest, most caring person I know. She's always filled me with countless words of wisdom over the years, but now being a mother myself, I look back and realise that she taught me the most incredible gift of all: to be like her and to be a good mum, to always be there and shower my little man with love through good and bad times. Looking back at everything my parents gave up, everything my mum did for us, well, it made me appreciate her so much more.

The best advice from other mothers I've been given is to slow down and embrace it all. Take in every moment – the good and the bad – as it goes by too quickly!

HAPPINESS IS . . .

Family! When it comes to happiness, my nearest and dearest really matter the most.

LA

'You can have it all, you just can't have it all at the same time.'

TAMMIN SURSOK

MOTHER TO PHOENIX, ACTRESS, SINGER, FILMMAKER, DESIGNER, ENTREPRENEUR, JUGGLER

'My biggest struggle is perfectionism. I want to be perfect all the time – the perfect mum, wife, actress, everything. I think that really gets to me.'

My mantra for myself and other mothers is: 'You can have it all, you just can't have it all at the same time'. The minute I accepted that, my whole life changed. I spent a lot of time in the beginning as a new mum feeling so guilty that I would leave my daughter Phoenix to go to work … and then feeling equally guilty that I wanted to work when Phoenix was around. You just have to be present in the moment and be grateful and not expect everything to be perfect all at once.

My life has always been dominated by work, so to suddenly stop that and become a mum was a hard transition at first. I felt like I lost a little bit of my identity for a while. However today, four years later, I feel like more of a real mum. I think I know what I'm doing a bit more now!

BLOGGING

I want to always come from a place of truth where motherhood is concerned. I started my website bottleandheels.com because I felt quite alone, isolated and lost as a new mum because I didn't have any friends with kids at the time. So I decided to create something where women could come together and talk about their struggles, journeys and triumphs so we could uplift each other. I think it has been successful because everything I do is authentic. Even when I talk about the struggles, pain and failures I've had, I try to write about it in a relatable way.

THE JUGGLE

My biggest struggle is perfectionism. I want to be perfect all the time – the perfect, mum, wife, actress, everything. I think that really gets to me. I think that's drawn from celebrity and the media in a way, and then before you know it, you're struggling. I'm getting better, though. I think therapy and self-awareness is very important for everyone. Everyone has something that can be helped through another person's training.

Of course it's not always smooth sailing! I

'My definition of success is happiness, freedom, gratitude and giving back.'

remember being in a large bookshop once and Phoenix had a poo explosion! At that moment someone asked for a picture of me and I was like, 'Um I can't do this right now!' It was very inopportune timing.

THE EARLY DAYS

My first acting role was *Home and Away* back in 2000 when I was just sixteen. When I was younger there were times when I would forget my lines. Even though everyone forgets their lines, it's always a little embarrassing. However, I've now been in this business for so long that now I can just look at a script and remember it. It's not so bad anymore!

My career path has been a great ride. After I finished *Home and Away*, I moved to LA where I got a huge break by scoring a regular role on *The Young and the Restless* for two years. I then also starred in *Hannah Montana* alongside Miley Cyrus. Miley is even more feisty than people imagine! She's actually really talented and a really sweet girl, but kind of wild. I also starred in *Pretty Little Liars* for eight years. This year we wrapped the last ever episode.

FILMING *WHALING*

Filming *Whaling* was fantastic. Tom Felton, who also starred in the Harry Potter films, is just great. I had such a good time on set that I would think, 'this is very surreal'. I have to pinch myself to remember how I got there in the first place. Phoenix was on set quite a bit, but she was fine with it. My parents flew in to help out and she enjoyed being around the whole family.

FINDING LOVE

I met my husband on a film set ten years ago. He was the director. It's been a great love story ever since. You have to put work into marriage but it's been the best decision of my life.

I knew he was the one when I kissed him and felt electric shocks throughout my entire body! I really like how he was so super talented. I rang my mum and said I want to marry this guy because I just want to be part of his world.

GIVING BACK

When I first heard about ABC Reading Eggs Junior, I really wanted to be involved because I think education is so important from a very young age, especially when it comes to reading. I wanted to make sure that reading was also fun and exciting so Reading Eggs Junior was the perfect fit for Phoenix as it's specifically for kids aged two to four. She just loves the animations, games and electronic books. She's learning so much and it's really helped spark her interest even more in books. Her favourites are *The Giving Tree*, *The Cat and the Caterpillar* and *The Airport Book*. I don't allow screen time during the week so she uses the app on the weekend.

RAISING A DAUGHTER

I want Phoenix to feel like she has her own voice and to be an individual. I want her to know that she can fight for whatever she wants and that there's no dream she can't achieve. I also want her to know that being a woman is really powerful and it's up to her to make her own destiny.

'I want Phoenix to feel like she has her own voice and to be an individual.'

IT'S EXHAUSTING IN THE MOST WONDERFUL WAY.

SCARLETT JOHANSSON

MELISSA ODABASH

SWIMWEAR DESIGNER, MOTHER OF TWO DAUGHTERS

'Children are amazing, they keep everything in reality and they are not impressed by anything you have achieved or won or any press you have received. They keep you grounded.'

I grew up in New Jersey in the United States, so I was basically outside all the time playing sports. My childhood was so simple looking back at it – it was easy: you played with your neighbours and friends, there were no computers or mobile phones, unlike nowadays.

I began my career modelling in Italy and shooting a lot of swimwear with different brands. I was very sporty so I was booked a lot for swimwear shoots and I finally decided, after not liking any of the garments that I was modelling, that I was going to design my own collection. Everyone at the time was only designing prints, so I wanted to do a line of just solid colours, which I thought was missing in the industry.

I started in Italy and no one spoke any English, so I learned Italian and started making a sample line which I began selling to the other models. I would also go door to door selling to people I met. After two years my friend Barrie, who still works with me today, took my samples to New York and managed to get them featured in *Sports Illustrated*. This was my very first shoot with Tyra Banks, Heidi Klum and Naomi Campbell. After this, I slowly got my products sold in department stores and built my company to where I am today.

Throughout my career, nothing has ever come easy. Retail is such a difficult industry and no one warns you of what might happen, because nobody really knows. But now I love it and I sell in sixty countries around the world. Even today I face some of the same struggles and some new ones, but you just learn to deal with them, and dealing with them gets easier and calmer.

THE JUGGLE

I met my husband and after three months I fell pregnant. At the time I was still modelling and selling my swimwear. I worked every day throughout my pregnancy, right up until the day my first daughter was born. This was also the time when I moved from Rome to London. I remember having some of my boxes that needed to be shipped brought to the hospital because they were urgent. The nurse came in and I had red, blue and yellow bikini piles all over the bed. Women have to learn very quickly how to multitask and although it's not easy, it has to be done. Especially when juggling a career and a family. But I am a very calm person and I have made it work. Family will always come first and I don't think I have ever had a day off!

SOCIAL MEDIA

I love social media for some things. It is so hard to start a company without much money and it is so important to create brand awareness. With social media like Instagram, it's made it easier. It's a great tool to boost your overall brand awareness – it's such an amazing free tool to use to get your brand out there. I could never afford an advertisement in *Vogue*, so I used other tools to help me promote the brand. I also had to create brand awareness by travelling and meeting people, creating a network in order to help my brand. This is a much longer and harder road to take for any company, but you learn a lot from it and it can still be very rewarding.

MY FAMILY LIFE

Unless you have had a baby, there is just no way to explain it. It is such a magical and happy time. But it is also a huge responsibility that for the rest of your life, you need to take care of them and always put their life before yours. For me, the biggest challenge is knowing when to give them more freedom. I have two daughters and I'm very possessive with them both. I love hanging out with them and spending as much time as possible with them. Having travelled the world as a model at such a young age, I had to grow up so quickly, which is the reason why I feel I need to protect their childhood.

Children are amazing, they keep everything in reality and they are not impressed by anything you have achieved or won or any press you have received. They keep you grounded. My two daughters (one of whom is a young teenager), are more interested in where they are going on their next vacation and how much pocket money they will get. They are also the best at giving me opinions on things including my designs. They often say 'no way, don't put that in your collection.' They are two of my most important muses!

FAMILY TIME

We love spending time together as a family and I love my time with my daughters. On holidays we often go to my house in Florida and visit my mum. This is one of my favourite vacations because we chill, do sports, go fishing, go rollerblading and go to the gym together. I only have one friend there so it's total family time. I now also take my eldest daughter on work trips with me so she can help out and it's a great experience for her.

HEALTHY LIVING

My health and wellbeing is very important to me. I don't like alcohol and never have, I have never smoked and maintaining a healthy lifestyle is essential. I try to stick to an alkaline-based diet because that's what is best for my body. I also love jogging as it helps me clear my mind after a busy day. I try to walk or cycle everywhere as well, as this keeps me active. I take my daily vitamins and drink lots of water, which also helps my body. Personally, I also think that taking time for yourself is important to your wellbeing, so I go and get a massage once a week. You should never take advantage of your health because it is everything and so important!

BEING A GIRL BOSS

Over the course of my career I have been so lucky to have many achievements, I have won many awards and each time I think, 'ahh I'm finally there', then the next year something more amazing comes along. I think my proudest achievement has been winning the Humanitarian Award. It was by far the best because it meant the most to me. It was about me as a person not as a designer. I am truly honoured to have such an amazing award!

Recently I got a call for a special order and although I have worked with some of the top celebrities and the royal family, this order made me so happy. It was for Barbra Streisand, who I love. She is such an icon, I was just so excited! I told all the girls in my office but they are all in their twenties so they didn't really understand why I was so excited. This has been the most recent highlight!

THREE THINGS THAT MAKE ME SMILE . . .

My kids, my family and my friends.

MY BIGGEST ROLE MODEL IS . . .

My mother. She is incredibly supportive, has amazing taste and she taught me everything. She is so chic and my passion flourished when I was young when she used to buy me bikinis from Saint Martin every year, where she used to holiday with my father. That was always my big gift and I have her to thank for all of my successes. She has also always given me the best advice when I was growing up and throughout my career. She told me to always be positive, be kind and never say you can't do something.

HAPPINESS IS . . .

Being healthy!

Photography by: Bartek Szmigulski

NOËLLA COURSARIS MUSUNKA

INTERNATIONAL MODEL, PHILANTHROPIST, MOTHER OF TWO

'It truly goes beyond words to have healthy children after such a process and meet the babies you've already loved for months. To hold them for the first time is magical.'

I was born in the Democratic Republic of the Congo, but after my father died when I was five, my mother sent me to Europe to live with family as she couldn't afford to look after me alone. I struggled growing up and had a tough upbringing, but focused on my education and eventually grew into the person I am today.

A friend of mine entered me into a competition for Agent Provocateur, which I won, so I then went on to shoot my first campaign with them. I was definitely nervous to shoot for such a globally known brand so early on in my career, but that is how my modelling career began.

EMPOWERING CONGOLESE GIRLS

In 2007 we started Malaika, a grassroots non-profit that focuses on girls' education, empowerment and community programs. The foundation operates in Kalebuka, a village thirty minutes away from my hometown of Lubumbashi. At the beginning, we only had a few classrooms and had to work hard to engage the community. Today, we have a dedicated team of Congolese staff and a network of passionate pro bono professionals from around the world who donate their time and expertise. We work with the village to create community-driven change, and we are all united by our belief in the human right to education for both boys and girls. Over the years, we have grown tremendously, and have built a complete school and community centre. In addition to providing 314 girls with an education, we now operate seventeen wells that provide more than 30,000 people with clean water annually, run a thriving agricultural project that helps feed the students and teaches the community about organic farming and offer vocational classes and recreational sports programs. Our model village can be duplicated anywhere – we started with just a vision and now have over 300 students, eager to shake up the world! Each year we add a new grade and classroom.

We provide our students with a quality, holistic education and many of our students continue to earn high marks on the national exam, proving the strength of our curriculum. These girls would likely have been left at home without opportunities in their future, so our mission is to provide them with a foundation by which they can build the lives they dream of for themselves.

My career highlight has definitely been laying the first brick for the school in Kalebuka. It was a momentous occasion for me. On a personal level, it was in that moment that everything started to feel incredibly real and tangible. We had helped many young girls before that point, but that first brick symbolised the potential to impact so many more lives, helping to raise the future female leaders of tomorrow.

THE GLOBAL FUND TO FIGHT AIDS

The Global Fund read about the work was doing and reached out. I was reluctant to accept at first because when I attach my name to something, I have to be able to commit 100 per cent – being a mother, modelling and running Malaika are already full-time responsibilities. I had to carefully consider the level of input I could have. Ultimately, my decision came down to the incredible number of people the Global Fund helps every day and the lives I could impact by working with them. There was no way I could say no. The Global Fund is an amazing organisation that was started by Bill and Melinda Gates, together with Kofi Annan. I admire their ethos and all that they've done. In the Democratic Republic of the Congo, more than 400 children under the age of five die every day from malaria and that struck me. If I can use my voice to bring awareness, I have to do it.

EXPANDING MY FAMILY

Two days after my wedding I discovered I was pregnant. We were moving from the UK to Germany for my husband's work, so I was surrounded by boxes, doing a bit of modelling and volunteering full-time to grow Malaika. I had JJ in Germany, which was a long, difficult birth. But to finally hold him was such an overwhelmingly beautiful moment. Now eight years old, James Jr, who we call JJ, is my sunshine! With my daughter, Cara, I had a water birth, which was quicker. It truly goes beyond words to have healthy children after such a process and meet the babies you've already loved for months. To hold them for the first time is magical.

THE JUGGLE

Going back to work wasn't too much of a struggle for me. My mind always needs to be busy and I multi-task between my kids, husband, house, Malaika, philanthropic endeavours and modelling, and a lot of things I do behind the scenes to help people or other projects. But I do make time to relax by going to the gym, the spa or just reading. It's very important to find time to take care of yourself.

Of course, nobody can prepare you for being a mother. It's not something you learn, and though it comes naturally, the first few months can be hard, with many nights of disrupted sleep and no routine established at the beginning. My son had trouble sleeping the first few months and then he was fine, but my daughter Cara would wake up several times a night until she was two years old. With her, I had to take a step back from modelling, as I really wanted to be there for her and my family. I didn't have my parents around me growing up, so for me, as a mother, it's a priority to be present for my children. Everything revolves around their well-being. I make sure I secure time each day for my children and husband, and time for work. Finding a balance can be difficult, but I focus on my children when they're getting ready for school and in the evenings for dinner, helping with their homework and reading to them before bed. When my children are at school, I hold Skype calls, discuss the day's events at the Malaika school with our Congolese or New York-based team, and handle various aspects of our non-profit with the international team.

'Of course, nobody can prepare you for being a mother. It's not something you learn, and though it comes naturally, the first few months can be hard.'

'It's important to take time for yourself. It will always help you to be a calm and patient parent.'

MUM ADVICE

I didn't grow up with my mother, so I didn't receive advice growing up. But, getting to know her as an adult, she has been incredibly supportive of all the work I do and is an excellent grandmother to my children. The best advice I've received is to enjoy every second of being a parent as time flies. I can't believe my son is already eight years old and in school and my daughter is starting school as well. You have to appreciate all of it because children truly do grow up quickly!

My advice to other mums is that it's important to take time for yourself. It will always help you to be a calm and patient parent, more centered and purposeful. And when you are with the kids, you must be present – kids love stories, games and attention, and will always notice when their parents aren't fully engaged! You learn so much through their eyes and their imagination. I learn a lot from my kids, but I always aim to advise them the best I can throughout their lives. Sometimes they're sad about situations not working out now they wanted, which happens to us all, but I always explain that life works in funny ways and it has its ups and downs and sometimes you win and other times you lose – but it all has a wonderful way of working out.

HAPPINESS IS . . .

Having healthy children and seeing our students and their families prospering and being well.

MY MOTTO IS . . .

Use your voice. Everyone has the ability to change the course of their lives and those around them, but it all starts with conviction and a lot of passion.

adidas

LINDY RAMA-ELLIS

CREATIVE DIRECTOR, MOTHER OF FOUR

'My mother always taught me that a loving, nurturing home environment is provided for by hard work, strong work ethic and self sacrifice.'

My childhood was incredible. I was surrounded by so much love! My happiest memories are of being with my grandparents at their holiday home. We would spend our days fishing and playing board games. I grew up in Tasmania so I was totally free. I would spend all day, every day outside.

I have definitely faced so many challenges in my time. Twenty years ago when I was modelling, Asian models were not used very much, so I unfortunately I didn't really get the 'big' jobs back then. When they were used, it was always to portray a very different image from the diverse one we know today. I developed a thick skin and a wider perspective early on. When it comes to setbacks, I live by the mantra; 'Always look forward, never look back.'

CAREER

A highlight of my career would be walking in Mercedes-Benz Fashion Week Australia for the fashion show of one of my closest friends, Toni Maticevski. Such good memories and such a fun time in my life. The pinnacle would be landing collaborative roles with Louis Vuitton, La Mer and Omega, among others. Such strong reputable brands that want me as a partner is an incredible journey.

Fashion has always been part of my life in some way or another. So, for me, fashion design was the next step on from modelling. It's very new to me so I'm still learning, and growing every day! I'm definitely inspired by my travels. I LOVE to travel. I absolutely adore being immersed in different cultures.

'Be kind in everything to everyone.'

CURRENT JUGGLE

At the moment I have Rama Voyage, my fashion label that specialises in destination wear. I'm an ambassador for a newly launched app called Peanut that helps mums connect with like-minded mums. I also work closely as a partner with Omega and the prestige skincare brand La Mer. All the brands I work with at the moment I believe in wholeheartedly.

FAMILY LIFE

Juggling work and my first child was incredibly difficult, but fortunately for me I had started my own business with my ex-husband and could work from home. I can remember having to breastfeed in the bathroom cubicle or other obscure places when we needed to do trade shows. Tiredness makes even the most disorganised mind become more efficient. But I definitely enjoyed being back at work. It was important to me to work again. It was good for my mental state, even though it was just about the hardest thing I ever did.

Now with four children, like any working mum it's just about time management. I need everything to run like clockwork but it doesn't always go to plan. Like the times I get the call from school with sick kids, there is nothing you can do because the children always come first. Any plan or schedule for that day becomes swallowed up. But I learned to deflect and not give up, so I would switch to a phone meeting rather than face to face, for example. Where possible, adapt and continue. So, it starts with plans and processes and when the wheels fall off, just adapt to whatever works. The biggest challenge is patience. I am always in a rush and I don't enjoy slowing down but with the children patience is critical!

A typical day really depends if I'm traveling for work or not, but if I'm home in Bali it starts with a 6.15 a.m. wake-up, driving the kids to the Green School in Bali (a one and a half hour round trip), followed by gym, eggs, then all day working, a smoothie on school pick-up, then after-school activities. We usually like to end the day with a beach walk or swim, then wind down for bedtime.

At home we have an age range from seven months to twelve years so when we are altogether we love hanging out in the pool or exploring beaches. Down time is important, too, with my kids. After sport and play dates, I like the kids to recharge their batteries with time just resting up at home. Right now, we have two in the pool, one resting in bed and one making a cake! Pretty standard.

LESSONS FROM MY MOTHER

My mother always taught me that a loving, nurturing home environment is provided for by hard work, strong work ethic and self-sacrifice.

The best advice I have for other mums is to be kind to yourself, and remember that most mothers find it hard. People talk about 'finding balance' as if it is a light switch. It certainly isn't. It takes practice and finding a happy point may take many attempts of trial and error. I guess my advice to friends would be to find the closest baby–work–sleep–life-partner successful juggling act that works for you and try to refine it.

THINGS I WANT TO TEACH MY KIDS ARE . . .

To be kind in everything to everyone.

THINGS THAT MAKE ME SMILE ARE. . . .

My kids. Stupid videos on the internet. Gucci bags.

HAPPINESS IS . . .

Seeing the sun in Melbourne. Sometimes it's there all day. Sometimes it's not there but always peeping out around the clouds. If it isn't there today it will be soon enough. Just hold on and soon the warm touch of the sun will be on your face again.

A MOTHER'S LOVE FOR HER CHILD IS LIKE NOTHING ELSE IN THE WORLD. IT KNOWS NO LAW, NO PITY, IT DARES ALL THINGS AND CRUSHES DOWN ON ALL THAT STANDS IN ITS PATH.

AGATHA CHRISTIE

Photography by FishFayce.com

CAROLINE STANBURY

LADY OF LONDON, MOTHER OF THREE

'Things that make me smile are my children, my husband and my work. I look up to hard working mums and women who can juggle a marriage, family and work life, a real modern role model.'

My childhood was spent at home in a large country estate. I remember us always being together and surrounded by friends and family. When starting out in my career, I was able to really inspire myself. I wanted to earn my own money, simple as that really!

BECOMING A MUM

When I had my first born, Yasmine, I was a stylist. And then with the twins, Zack and Aaron, I had Gift Library (my former business selling high-end gifts). I had chosen to do IVF and at the time was building a big business, and suddenly I had to do it all at the same time. It wasn't easy but it is possible. I had a good team around me, both in my family and business. Meeting my kids for the first time was so life-changing. They don't come with a manual so at first all you want to do is sleep! I had a very long labour, but once you get your head around it all and the life change, you just can't stop staring at them. The biggest challenge for me was juggling Gift Library, *Ladies of London* (the television show on Bravo TV) and family life. It was hard and stressful, and you want to do everything well.

THE JUGGLE

Babies don't need a lot of attention: when they are young, all they want to do is sleep, so it's getting them into a routine that's key. I was lucky enough that I had a good maternity nurse. You can take a baby everywhere with you but it's when their personalities start to develop that it becomes harder – especially with three children. They want to grow and go off in different directions. When you have a business and you're juggling that with babies and home life, you just get on with it. In terms of maternity leave, I had a big business, so I didn't have the luxury of taking leave. I think I went back to work around one week after giving birth! I breastfed Yasmine, so she would be brought to the office for feeding times. Going back to work wasn't a difficult decision, it's just what you have to do. You can't just leave people who rely on you. I had an office of people relying on me!

Photography by Capital D Studio, Meredith Damouni

'Juggling children and career continues to be very hard and you never know if you're doing it right or not.'

Juggling children and career continues to be very hard and you never know if you're doing it right or not. For my work, I have to travel a lot. That's how it's always been so the children have grown up with me not working at home – it's their norm. It does make me feel guilty and I probably do overcompensate when I am back.

We try to spend loads of time together as a family. We have movie night every Friday religiously. The children all sleep over in our room, they love it. We go on family days out, and beach days too! Living in Dubai has made it very easy to spend time together, as it's very outdoorsy and fun for children, and it's easy to find things to do. But they're getting older and Yasmine wants to spend more time with her friends.

LADIES OF LONDON

Somebody put me forward for the television show *Ladies of London*. Two or three people actually suggested me and I really wasn't expecting to get through. It was by complete accident. At first, I wasn't sure whether to do it or not. I went for a screen test and I was first to be chosen. It was a complete shock!

UPS AND DOWNS

My proudest achievement has been bringing up all three of my children. I think they have grown to be very polite and well adjusted. Gift Library and *Ladies of London* are also among my top achievements. In terms of challenges, there have been so many. Keeping Gift Library afloat was definitely one of them. It's easier to raise money for an idea than it is to keep the idea going. Hiring a good team, going through CVs, finding the right people with the right attitude – those are all challenging. Having faith in people for doing the jobs you can't, and relying on them. Also doing the TV show and being petrified of what people might think of you and scared that people might not like you. That was definitely a challenge!

SUCCESS

Success to me is when I look around at what I have and am truly happy. Success is not about money but about being content with what you have. When I was younger I used to think it was all about the money you made, but really it's about managing everything well, business and family. The biggest career highlight for me was being in *The Financial Times*.

LESSONS FROM MY MOTHER

My mother taught me strength, character, to have a stiff upper lip and to not let things break you. If at first you don't succeed, try and try again.

MOTHER DUTY

As a mother, the best advice I've been given is to not worry too much about how you're going to bring your children up. It's instinct. We're all winging it and every child is different, someone else's will not be like mine. Mother's intuition is always best, and you have to follow your own path.

HAPPINESS IS . . .

Being at home in my family bubble.

'The best advice I've been given is to not worry too much about how you're going to bring your children up. We're all winging it.'

JUST BECAUSE YOU BECOME A MOTHER, IT DOESN'T MEAN YOU LOSE WHO YOU ARE.

BEYONCÉ KNOWLES-CARTER

LAURA CSORTAN

TV PRESENTER, TRAVELLER, MUM

'Being a single mum is all consuming, but amazing! I just take it one day at a time and focus on being the best mum I can.'

I spent my childhood outdoors. My family were very 'outdoorsy' and we had a shack at Marion Bay in South Australia's Yorke Peninsular. It was a very modest little place with a boat and diving gear, which was all we needed to keep us entertained from sunrise to sunset. We also had a place on the Murray River where we water-skied. I can't ever remember a time where we weren't active!

PATH TO SUCCESS

I was studying a Bachelor of Applied Science at the University of South Australia when a model scout approached me. Not long after that, the same agent entered me into Miss Universe Australia. Long story short, I won! This opportunity propelled me into the entertainment world. It was exciting, not to mention a very steep learning curve. Miss Universe Australia wasn't really recognised like it is now – I had to pave my own way. I worked very hard at gaining knowledge of the industry, often working for free to sharpen up on my presenting and producing skills. I knocked on a lot of doors until I got my first big gig hosting a show for the Travel Channel in the US. This saw me travel the world and ultimately allowed me to put together a showreel, which I would later submit to Channel Seven for the role of presenter on *The Great Outdoors*. I auditioned against 800 others for the coveted position, and after a series of screen tests and meetings, I finally secured the role. What a dream job it was! I did many laps of the globe for almost eight amazing years. I then went on to co-host *Wheel of Fortune* with Larry Emdur. A series of other shows followed, including a role as sports presenter on the desk of Fox Sports news. A career highlight was working with National Geographic recently to film a movie, which saw me ride a motorbike across North Africa through the Sahara desert!

THE JUGGLE

After travelling the globe and being carefree for so many years, getting pregnant meant my life did a total

'I want to teach her kindness, integrity, honesty, to be hard working and loving.'

backflip! I had been travelling the world at a cracking pace, being able to pick up and leave whenever and however I liked. All this came to a screeching halt with my pregnancy, which floored me – I suffered from severe hyperemesis, so I was in and out of hospital for pretty much the whole pregnancy.

Meeting my daughter for the first time is the most difficult thing to describe. It was a moment that was overwhelming and utterly exciting. It was an immediate intense love and a life-changing experience. Being a single mum is all-consuming, but amazing! I just take things one day at a time, and focus on being the best mum I can. I was certainly ready for the challenge when she arrived.

I am a very hands-on mum. Layla Rose is almost two years old and I still breastfeed and co-sleep with her. I've turned down a lot of work opportunities, particularly those that involve travel, but I figure Layla is only a baby for such a short amount of time and I want to spend it with her. I do miss the excitement that comes with filming great stories abroad, but it will happen again once she's older. She is all that matters right now. I write from home and do local TV appearances that I can manage, mostly with Layla in tow.

RETURNING TO WORK

My first shoot was when Layla was just three weeks old. She was with me the whole time. I breastfed while I was in hair and make-up, and had my mum there to hold her while I presented. It felt great to work and finally get dressed up, and do my hair and make-up after so long. I was also happy to get home and put my PJs back on!

The biggest challenge is definitely the juggle of it all. Making sure the little one is happy and healthy; making sure I am happy and healthy so I can continue to give to her. Sometimes it seems almost impossible to leave the house, but regardless of how you feel, you just have to keep going. I support her entirely on my own so work is definitely important. I generate an income for us both to live on.

LESSONS FOR MY DAUGHTER

I want to teach her kindness, integrity, honesty, to be hard-working and loving.

CHRISELLE LIM

DIGITAL ENTREPRENEUR, MOTHER

'At first I wasn't sure how to do this whole mommy thing and it felt so foreign to me. It took me a few weeks but after that, I didn't know what life was like before!'

I spent most of my childhood by myself in my room. I loved reading, writing, creating, playing music and daydreaming in my own little world. I've always been a bit more introverted and really enjoyed my time on my own. I was always very independent!

MY CAREER

Before I became as a stylist, and went on to become an editor at a local luxury magazine called *Genlux*, I was on the traditional fashion-editor path. Then eight years ago I met Michelle Phan who introduced me to the digital world. At that point, you were either on YouTube or you had a blog. I noticed that there really wasn't anyone doing fashion on YouTube, so I uploaded my first video and the response was insane – I had 500,000 views overnight! I saw a need and want for this kind of curated, elevated content, so I ran with it. From there I started The Chriselle Factor, which became a success due to a combination of hard work, right timing and the unique content we were posting. I later started my company Chriselle INC. so I spent a lot of time in the office with my team or I was travelling every other week to a different country for work! It was a very fast-paced life!

MEETING MY DAUGHTER

When I met Chloe for the first time I was incredibly excited, but at the same time scared. I wasn't sure how to do this whole mommy thing and it felt so foreign to me. It took me a few weeks to bond with my baby, but after that, I didn't know what life was like before!

THE JUGGLE

The biggest challenge for me is the guilt that comes as a working mother. Even though we know we are doing this work for our growing families, it's hard to escape the guilt. I've talked to many women about it, and we all say the same thing: 'Maybe I'll get out of it, it's only my first year in.' At least for me, there is a never-ending cycle of feeling guilty when I have to leave my family and travel for work. It feels good to be in this position and have a sense of freedom, but it's easy to feel guilty about loving it.

Since having a child I now feel like I have more control over my life. At first it was chaotic of course, but once I realised I had to prioritise and set boundaries for everything, it forced me to get more organised and find the right people to help me out. Although I'm busier than ever, I'm able to get more done now than before I had my daughter. I now know where to allocate my time and where to delegate. I'm able to really be present and not get distracted by things. Work is work and family time is family time … no if, ands or buts!

BACK TO WORK

One of the upsides of running your own business is that you can control and create your own schedule, but also that is one of the downfalls as well. Because I was the face of my business and brand, I felt a lot of pressure (from myself) to jump back in immediately. I took about a month off and started working soon after that, but I was able to work from home. My team would come to my house and we would all get work done together. I had an

'My definition of success is when you have the freedom to do what you love, with the people that you love.'

incredible support team to help me out during this time. So many of us focus on goal-setting and finding work–life balance, but there comes a point where you have to let it go and enjoy the ride. There will always be seasons where your work life is going to be heavier, and other times when life takes over – you can have it all, but not at the same time. You have to be realistic and know that there are going to be seasons for everything.

I'm also a huge proponent for spending quality time over quantity, and it's hard to truly connect with people when you are tied to your phone, so we have a 'no phone' policy after 6 p.m. at the house. I might sneak in a little Instagram story with my daughter Chloe here and there, but I try to keep it off and away. I also physically turn off and go on a digital detox from time to time. I think it's so important to disconnect from the world so you can truly connect with yourself. Chloe loves drawing and painting, so when we unwind, we usually have a family paint day! Lately she has been really curious about birds so we got some bird houses and painted them. She gets so excited when she sees the birds eating their food out of the birdhouse she made for them! She also LOVES music and dancing so almost every night after dinner we will just turn up her favourite songs and dance for a few minutes before bath time!

HEALTHY LIVING

It took me a full year to completely lose all of the baby weight. Honestly, the most important thing is to be patient! Someone told me it took you nine months to create this baby, give yourself the same amount of time to lose the weight! I drank a detox smoothie and Korean seaweed soup (which is great for healing and restoring your body) almost every day for a year. I didn't start working out until three months after delivery and even then, I was very mild with my workouts. You need to build yourself back up instead of jumping right back into it. I have an amazing personal trainer who focuses on prenatal fitness. I see her two to three times a week and besides that I stay pretty active with my toddler, who still wants me to hold her everywhere we go!

Self-care is essential to me and is one of the ways I bring sanity and peace back into my crazy, chaotic, creative life! I feel the most balanced when I take care of my mind, body and soul, so I set the intention to do things that make me feel great physically; like exercising, daily meditation, getting a facial once a month and a massage once a week. I probably spend a good fifteen minutes in the morning and fifteen minutes at night just prepping my skin. In Korean culture, there are anti-aging products, of course, but it's not like in the States. There, skincare is a lifestyle from the day you are born.

GIRL BOSSES

I look up to women who have built businesses and were able to impact and inspire their community along the way. Sheryl Sandberg being one of them.

MY PROUDEST ACHIEVEMENT HAS BEEN . . .

Being able to build my business and career, all while raising a strong, resilient toddler and family! My career highlight has been launching my own fashion collection with Nordstrom.

MY DEFINITION OF SUCCESS IS . . .

When you have the freedom to do what you love, with the people that you love. When you wake up every morning excited to build something! When you find your calling and purpose and are ready to fulfil that purpose.

LESSONS FROM MY MOTHER

My mother taught me that the bigger the opportunity that has been given to you, the more responsibility you have to society. To always give back what has been given to you.

BEST ADVICE I'VE BEEN GIVEN IS . . .

Days are long but years are short! Every phase your toddler is going through will pass, don't sweat it too much. And sleep!

HAPPINESS IS . . .

Being content with where I am in life, and being fully present and connected with my mind, body and soul.

CHRISTIANE DUIGAN

CO-FOUNDER OF BODYISM, MOTHER OF THREE

'My biggest achievement definitely has to be my three children and the labour of bringing them in to this world.'

I spent my childhood living between Brazil and Australia watching my parents run their business. I didn't realise it at the time but I was learning so much about business, people, the importance of integrity and an eye for detail.

I had worked a few jobs in childcare before I met my inspirational husband, James. I used to watch him get up every day at 5 a.m., train clients until 7 a.m. and then write books in the evening. But what struck me, besides his work ethic, was that it all seemed like so much fun to him. As we began to work together, I saw the really important distinction between working hard and working smart. Especially when our beautiful children came into our lives; success began to look very different. It was more about quality time with the people we love. Before I had kids, I was helping grow our business Bodyism with James. I was very much involved with logistics and operations with our supplement and clothing brand. As we travelled, I ran the business from my laptop all around the world.

Since having children, in terms of my life outside of work, it's changed everything in ways that I could not have possibly imagined. It has expanded my heart and my love beyond anything I had ever dreamed of. As each new baby arrived into our family, that love just grew and has also deepened my love for my husband as I've watched him become a wonderful father. It has been so great for us to be such a powerful team both as parents and business partners. As for the business, it hasn't changed at all. As the business has grown, I've become much better at what I do and I can do it in a shorter amount of time. There have also been brilliant people in our team who I can delegate things to.

RETURNING TO WORK

Going back to work, there was an element of struggle. I love what I do but for every minute I spent away from the kids I struggled with guilt. I've learned to let go of that guilt and practice acceptance. Once I began to accept myself and the situation, things began to change much

'Be present to each moment because they really do grow up so fast. Breathe and find peace in the chaos.'

'To find the joy and love in everything I do.'

more easily. I found that I had a lot more time with my family and that I was much more present during those times, which was a beautiful thing. It's also lovely for the children to visit Bodyisms around the world to see what their mum and dad have created.

People management has been the biggest challenge in my career. Embracing that people will always do what's best for them and learning to encourage that has been a challenge, but incredibly rewarding. Our biggest lesson is the importance of watertight contracts and learning what motivates each person to get the best out of them.

Success to me is having the freedom and time to do what we want to do, when we want to do it and with the people who we love! To have a business we are proud of that does good things in the world, and a lifestyle filled with beautiful moments.

THE JUGGLE

To be honest, I don't feel like I'm juggling anything. I feel like I've found a lovely balance. These days, with three young children and my passion for being a mum, my time is swayed to be more with the family. I love creating experiences and adventures together – this is my idea of fun! It can be something simple like a game in the park or travelling somewhere new. James creates a great balance and makes sure we get plenty of resting time at home doing nothing, just being together and enjoying each other's company.

BOUNCING BACK

I have had very difficult pregnancies. I get very tired, sick and put on a lot of weight. But I never focused on it too much and just allowed my body to do what it was going to do. After my babies, my body falls back to the way it was after about a year, in a naturally healthy and happy way. My real joy comes from being a mother, wife and friend – not a number on a scale or dress size. In saying that, it's a lovely feeling to be able to get back in to my clothes again!

HEALTHY LIVING

I live by our five pillars of health. It's a very holistic and effective way of approaching wellness. It really creates a happy, balanced mindset rather than an obsessive one. When it comes to nutrition, I eat a balanced diet, mainly cutting out sugar, gluten and alcohol.

I move my body in different ways that I enjoy, from walks to classical ballet and Pilates. I truly believe in the power of the mind and as we say, 'any transformation that happens in the body, happens in the mind first'. The same goes for any aspect of your life. I love my sleep and my optimal amount is nine hours. You can find me with an eye mask and ear plugs in so that nothing or no one wakes me up! I also believe that I can change the way I am feeling in three simple deep breathes. Whether I'm feeling anxious about getting somewhere on time with three kids or when there are changes in the business.

THINGS THAT MAKE ME SMILE

The things that make me smile include watching my children play together, sharing a joyful moment with my husband and eating good food. My biggest achievement definitely has to be my three children and the labour of bringing them in to the world. I had three natural births with no drugs and these were the proudest, most incredible experiences of my life. Happiness to me is a state of mind. Happiness can be found anywhere at anytime. It's like a switch in your brain that can be turned on and off, so I choose to have it on as much as possible.

LESSONS FROM MY MOTHER

To find the joy and love in everything I do. I learned this from her mother and I hope I can pass on this same lesson to my children.

TEACH YOUR DAUGHTERS LESS ABOUT FITTING INTO GLASS SLIPPERS AND MORE ABOUT SHATTERING GLASS CEILINGS.

MELISSA MARCHIONNA

ZOE MARSHALL

TELEVISION AND RADIO HOST, MUM TO FOX

'It is such an out of body experience meeting your baby for the first time. I never thought I was maternal and now I certainly am!'

My childhood was wonderful. I had the best mum in the whole world. She separated from my dad when I was three, and now that I have my own child, I really understand and have so much respect for single mums. She just made it work. We lived with my grandmother on Sydney's North Shore for a while and my mum sometimes worked two jobs. She did everything for me. It was just such a happy, loving childhood with her. I sometimes think we were too close, perhaps even enmeshed, but she really was my best friend. I was always surrounded by family and cousins, and I would see my dad often too.

WHEN MY WORLD CHANGED

My mum was diagnosed with cancer when I was twenty years old. I knew from the moment she was diagnosed thatl wouldn't have her for very long. Our love was so deep and somehow I knew that I wouldn't have her forever.I think something in me knew from when she told me she was sick that I simply had to find a way to survive without her. I started going out, partying and distracting myself. When she passed, the feelings I experienced were unexplainable. The denial I had in place was so huge, it was a part of my survival. I've only just started to really feel she isn't here since I became a mum myself. Which is hard to understand because it's been twelve years since she passed. But my doula said something very profound to me that explained what I was going through. She said, 'When you give birth and become a mother, a mother is born. It's the one time you need your own mother again, to mother you.'

After Fox was born, I felt this huge void and a huge amount of grief. For a long time, I couldn't remember my mother's voice or see her face. It took me a good 10 years to remember her again. It's been beautiful to see her face again, but incredibly painful.

FINDING LOVE

I met Benji the old fashioned way – at a club! He was with a group of mates dancing, but it was really bad daggy dancing, and I thought in that moment he was definitely my kind of guy. He used a really bad pick-up line, 'You're a bit sexy.' And I replied, a little taken aback, 'Just a bit?' He laughed and said, 'No, I mean heaps sexy.' Smooth, right? And then he offered to buy me a drink. I said no, 'I can buy my own drinks!' We ended up sitting in a corner of the club talking for hours and I started falling quick.

He is quite a well-known footballer but I had no clue who he was. I think he was testing me because he told me he was a publisher, played soccer and had a daughter. I think he was trying to see if I'd stick around.

We instantly hit it off. Unfortunately his adopted father passed away very suddenly two months later. That was a massive turning point in our relationship. It definitely brought up so much of my grief and I just wanted to save him, but he had his own way of coping. We lost touch for a couple of months and then he resurfaced from his pain a few months later and the rest is history.

MEET THE MARSHALLS

Benji and I moved to Brisbane in 2017 as Benji was doing a year with the Broncos. It was there that we had a radio show called *Meet The Marshalls* on Nova Radio, which I absolutely loved doing. Working together was such a thrill. I had previously had two endometriosis removals and I was trying to fall pregnant. That was when I met Dr Shuguan Liu. His people reached out to me and asked if I would like to meet him. I didn't want to do his program (which meant fasting for two whole weeks!) but after listening to what he had to say and how brilliant he was I decided to do it. The radio show had ended and I had finished the first part of his treatment, which took three months (yes, not eating for over two weeks). Then the pregnancy program started and within six weeks of doing the treatment I found out I was pregnant. In fact, I was asked to be the host of *The House of Wellness* TV Show and found out I was pregnant all in the same weekend. But I was seriously committed to his program. I didn't want to go down the path of IVF until I had exhausted everything else. I also didn't want to go through another Brisbane summer! So Benji and I moved back to Sydney.

THE BIRTH

I had no idea what to expect from the birthing experience, but I had met an obstetrician who was a friend of a friend. I was very adamant that I didn't want any drugs and that I would not get induced. But Fox just didn't want to come out! I was doing everything I could to get the birth going. I was doing perennial massages, eating six dates a day, doing squats, eating curries, doing belly dancing in the living room, having sex – anything and everything to bring the labour on. I even spoke to Fox and told him it was time. I even did reverse psychology on him and that didn't help either! Finally I had my induction date booked in (the protocol at the private hospital I was with was when you go past forty weeks and ten days). We went to the hospital and it took an entire evening for the doctors to get a reading on what was going on with me. I got a few hours sleep when they woke me the next day with the obstetrician snapping on his gloves saying, 'lets get this show on the road.'

After trying stretch and sweeps, they used prostaglandin and then broke my waters, and still nothing. So they said they were going to induce me. They gave me medication called Syntocinon – it was my worst-case scenario. But I had done a 'she births course' and I was mentally ready for the good, bad and ugly.

I had pictures of my mum in the room, Benji had bought me red roses and my doula made a beautiful shrine – I even had fresh coconuts! I was fine for about two hours and then suddenly the contractions came on really, really strong. Sytocinon is like being on a treadmill and someone else is turning up the speed – but with contractions. Not ideal.

Benji was with me through every single one of them. My waters had broken so I was wearing a massive pad and disposable undies. I was attached to a drip (hard when trying to birth a baby and wanting to be active and move to labour) and the whole thing was just not what I envisioned. I had a bath and for two minutes I felt fantastic, and then I instantly hated it.

I got out of the bath and I began screaming. Primal screaming. I thought I was going to die. I broke down and cried nonstop. Benji broke down too, he could see I was broken. But he said the most beautiful words that kept me going. I did another eight hours and just when I wanted to give up, I pushed through. But it got really scary and brutal, and the whole moment felt very, very dark all of sudden. The midwife checked and I was only two centimetres dilated! That was when my soul shattered. All of that and two centimetres! I used many profanities and Benji knew it was time.

I screamed for the epidural. Which took an hour to be administered. NIGHTMARE. Then I had a rest. My body just opened up and Fox was born an hour later.

MEETING FOX

It is such an out-of-body experience meeting your baby for the first time. He was so beautiful. Benj was crying. I was crying. Then little Fox cried too. One thing I learned was to let him lead the way. And he did – he just simply latched on. It was the most incredible thing I'd ever seen – this little being finding his way to my boob and just suckling. I never thought I was maternal and now I certainly am!

POST BIRTH

I suffered from severe postnatal depletion, which is different to postnatal depression. It's a hormone imbalance where you feel very unwell all the time, you can't sleep, have flu symptoms and can't get well no matter what you try. It's pure exhaustion. I do think going back to work so soon was probably not the best thing for me, especially since Fox is exclusively breastfed. I would do a lot of things differently next time around, like prioritising my sleep and my wellness, and putting my health first.

THE JUGGLE

I am the co-host of *The House of Wellness* as well as the co-host of a national nightly radio show called *Celeb HQ* on Kiis FM. I think the best way to deal with the juggle is to have support in place. Teaching your baby how to sleep would be my number one! I've learned to rally the support. I struggled at first because I didn't have my mum but I realised that if I didn't have the support, then I needed to pay for help. It was impossible to do everything on my own, and to be a working mum too. The juggle is real! Find your partner again, too. Having sex is hard but reigniting the romance and having fun away from being a mum is vital. Enjoy time with friends, be kind to yourself. And sleep – when you can!

SOCIAL MEDIA

There are a lot of women doing a disservice by showing a curated version of motherhood. There's nothing that angers me more. I think we have a responsibly to show it 'all' and I think we should show there are so many 'not okay' moments. For me, I share things about motherhood and try to be transparent. I've had women reach out to me to say that I've become the mouthpiece for showing a real and raw side of motherhood. These women encourage me to show the realness because there's nothing more unjust than bullshitting people, and then going home and crying in your bed. Staying off social media is just as important for your sanity.

KIRSTEN WALKER

FOUNDER OF PALM BEACH COLLECTION, MOTHER OF TWO

'I believe having children has taught me so much about myself, how to be a better person, how to be patient and kind. Most importantly it has taught me how to look on the bright side when things get you down.'

We grew up on Sydney's northern beaches. We had a big property that encouraged us to embrace the outdoors and use our imagination. Two creeks, plenty of bush, endless amounts of flowers and Australian natives. It really was a wonderland. We spent most weekends playing in the garden or out on Pittwater having adventures on the boat.

My parents worked for themselves and my dad always created his own opportunities. As a result I have always been very inspired to create a product that meant something to people. When the opportunity came up for my brother and I to run our own business, I was really excited. I love a challenge. I had been a buyer at General Pants Group for ten years. The day after I gave my resignation to start Palm Beach Collection, I found out I was pregnant with my first baby.

EXPANDING THE FAMILY

Words cannot describe meeting my kids for the first time. It is true what they say, it is a love like no other. Absolutely love at first sight. The biggest challenge has been that I was never really able to switch off from work. I was back on my emails in the hospital only a few hours after the birth! But I am grateful for everything the business has given me and I wouldn't change it for the world.

My husband and I always said, 'Our kids will fit into our life,' but we quickly found out this wasn't the case at all! They don't fit into our life, we fit into theirs! Life has changed so much. There are the obvious things – never enough hours in the day, always thinking about other people before yourself, kids' parties rather than Sunday lunch with friends, however, I think the biggest change for me has been how I have grown as a person. Having children has taught me so much about myself; how to be a better person, how to be patient and kind. Most importantly it has taught me how to look on the bright side when things get you down; after all I have two healthy, happy children and so much to be grateful for. Having children can put pressure on relationships, I get that, but for my husband and me it has made us closer. We really have to have each other's back and I love that.

THE JUGGLE

Leaving my old job and finding out I was pregnant the day after I resigned was certainly an emotional challenge. I had nine months before things would change forever. I worked through my pregnancy with both kids and didn't take any maternity leave. Our office was at our house at that stage and I thought it would be easy! I think it was the hardest thing I have ever done. My kids weren't great daytime sleepers and I would spend an hour patting them to sleep, then they would sleep for maybe an hour and then be up again. Trying to breastfeed while entering orders, taking phone calls, answering emails . . . it was hard work. But at that stage the business was so young and needed my attention, so I had no choice. We couldn't afford to employ someone else and I didn't want to not be involved for nine months. Both my kids went to a home daycare at approximately nine months. After that, life became more manageable. I was lucky enough to have a fantastic support network around me and I couldn't have gotten through those early (and hard) days without the love and support of my husband and parents.

As time went on it did get easier. I think for families with both parents working, it's an ongoing battle and you never get the right balance. Dedicating certain times when you give your kids 100 per cent of your attention works for me. When I grab the kids from school, I am theirs until dinner most days. This helps ease the mother's guilt too (we all suffer from it).

GETTING BACK INTO SHAPE

First time around, the weight was a bit harder to shift. I think I was pretty shocked at what a challenge having a new baby was and then working on top of that. I didn't have or make the time for myself. I have always loved exercise so as soon as I started walking and running again, the weight came off. Second time around it happened a lot quicker. Having to chase around a very active toddler while managing a newborn and work, certainly helped. My tips would be to continue exercising throughout your pregnancy and just be kind to your body, look at what it has just done for you! Exercise and eat well, not because you hate your body, but because you love it.

FAMILY TIME

We are a pretty relaxed family. We love our days at the beach in the summer. Our kids love the water and we are all really happy by the sea. We recently put a pool in at home which was amazing over the summer. We really enjoy spending time at home, in the garden, reading, eating yummy food . . . just enjoying the slow life as our weekdays can be pretty busy and rushed.

WORKING MUM

If I have to answer an email or take a phone call, my kids understand now. I know some women might frown upon me working while I have my kids, but this is a way of life and my kids understand that if they want to continue living in Sydney, their mum and dad both need to work. I think it's important too that children see their mothers working. I am proud of my job and it's good for them to see that. After dinner and getting the kids to bed, I always check emails to see if anything needs attention. I actually don't mind working at night. It helps me get on top of my workload for the next day.

HEALTH AND WELLBEING

I try to be as healthy as I can but I don't beat myself up about it if I can't be as healthy as I would like. I used to be conscious about what I was eating and now after having kids I don't sweat it as much. I have always loved working out, yoga and particularly running, which means I am a pretty active person anyway. I want to be strong for my kids and have energy for them but I also want to enjoy the odd treat with them and teach them that everything is okay, in proportion!

MY ROLE MODEL

My role model is Mum; she is the most selfless and caring person, and nothing is ever a problem for her. She is always there for me when I need her, just as I hope to be for my kids. Mum has taught me to be kind, understanding, always give people another chance and the importance of family. Mum continues to teach me to not sweat the small stuff (still working on this). Growing up, my parents had their own business together. Mum did the books while my dad was out in the field manufacturing and selling.

etcetera

'Success is a happy and healthy family and to be surrounded by beautiful friends that make you laugh.'

Looking back now, I really see what a driving force my mum was for that business. Dad is the first to admit he could never have done it without her. Mum's experience in business has been instrumental with my company, Palm Beach Collection.

THE PALM BEACH COLLECTION

I have been so fortunate to travel for Palm Beach Collection, discovering new cities and meeting new people. You have to pinch yourself sometimes that this is work! Drawing inspiration from different cultures and having the opportunity to live like a local in other cities, such as Melbourne, is such a great part of what I do. I love an adventure.

I have had to learn lots of new skills since starting Palm Beach Collection. It's challenging to get out of your comfort zone and push yourself but at the same time, making mistakes is all a part of the learning process and I am so much better off for it now.

SUCCESS IS . . .

A happy and healthy family and to be surrounded by beautiful friends that make you laugh.

BEST ADVICE I'VE BEEN GIVEN AS A MOTHER

To listen to your gut instinct.

MY PROUDEST ACHIEVEMENT IS . . .

My children for sure.

THREE THINGS THAT MAKE ME SMILE . . .

My family, sunshine and the beach.

HAPPINESS IS . . .

My family and friends, the beach, good food and wine, and sunshine . . . oh, and maybe a new handbag!

TAHYNA TOZZI-MACMANUS

DIRECTOR, ACTRESS, MUM

'Everything has changed in the best possible way. Parenting is not easy and no doubt there will be days I am tested but overall a sense of contentment floods me when I look at our daughter. I look at the world through her eyes and try my best to make it a better place for her.'

I had an incredible childhood. I grew up with a supportive family and a mother who devoted her life to her girls. I remember playing in the backyard every afternoon, skateboarding to the beach to go surfing before a music class or Karate training. We were encouraged to do everything we wanted to do and not grow up too quickly.

ENTERING THE MODELLING WORLD

A common misconception about my sister and me is that we started a 'career' in modelling very young. In fact it was the opposite. Because my mother was a former model, she was often asked by photographer friends if my sister and I could be part of their shoots. She never let us go on our own and would never let us be in a position that we didn't feel comfortable with. We never entered any competitions, didn't get agents until our teenage years and truly didn't consider it a career opportunity until it actually played out that way. Certainly for myself I never took it that seriously because to be perfectly frank, I didn't think I looked like a model (I still don't). I was always creative, I was always performing. I was always a storyteller. Of course I took commercial and modelling work that came up, I would have been mad not to. I had always worked very hard though, something I learned from my mother. She engrained a certain professionalism in us, which I think most people found confronting. I remember shaking the hand of a magazine editor at age five and introducing myself. She asked which finishing school I went to, (a concept I had never heard of). I was just brought up that way. You introduce yourself, you behave and then you go home and play or do your homework.

THE ACTING WORLD

Again, acting was something that beautiful, famous people did. For me, it was something I did any chance I could because it is what I loved to do. Anyone who knew the twelve-year-old Tahyna would attest to this. If there was a stage, I was on it. Again, I never thought I could make a career from it until it happened. I was extremely fortunate to audition for an ABC series *Blue Water High* when I graduated high school. I landed that audition because the head of the production company at the time came to watch me perform in my high school musical after I convinced him I was capable of the gig. I got the role and worked very hard. I loved everything about being on a set and from that moment on I did everything in my power to learn all I could so I was able to do it for the rest of my life. I was a late bloomer so parties and boys came second to my dreams and the work that needed to go along with that.

I worked as a waitress and shop assistant to fund my education at a theatre company in New York after *Blue Water High* had finished. It really bugs me that actors and models are 'job shamed' for working other jobs to fund their dreams. I always embraced hard work and never took the easy route. Celebrity wasn't appealing to me – honest hard work was.

I challenged myself regarding my acting pursuits at the age of twenty-five. It was funny because my representation at the time put so much emphasis on my age and I was considered 'old'. It scared me that something I loved so deeply wasn't making me happy anymore. The industry is tough and for a certain period in my twenties, it took it's toll on me. I trusted a lot of people whom I had thought were friends but as it turned out, I was only of value if they thought they could gain something from me. I don't have a thick skin but certainly as I approached my thirties, I was able to see things for what they were. I knew deep down that my passion was always to be a storyteller, but it took a lot of hard lessons and relentless courage to finally be able to pursue the other side of storytelling in writing and directing.

I staged a production of John Patrick Shanley's *Savage in Limbo* that I directed with a group of actor friends in Los Angeles. The production sold out and from that moment on, it was like a slow-burning fire in the pit of my stomach suggesting that maybe I was meant for more than just performing. I started writing and directing my own films, and pushed myself further to educate myself.

It all snowballed from there, but each day I had to make the choice to work for it. It is easy to assume that a teenager who seemingly 'fell' into a career in front of the camera has a sense of entitlement and doesn't comprehend the luck. I do, but it certainly didn't come easily. I had a lot to prove and still continue to work with that mentality. Nothing has ever been handed to me on a silver platter. My career has played out exactly as it should and for the first time in my life, I genuinely feel deserving of what I have achieved and I know I have so much more I want to do. I'm definitely not done yet.

FALLING IN LOVE

I met my husband at that point in my life where I was going through that transition. I was twenty-five, I had been a serial monogamous relationship kind of girl and boyfriends had never worked out because I was so focused on my career. He was different though, it's hard to explain. I was introduced by a dancer friend of mine in Los Angeles. Tristan was a professional dancer on the US version of *Dancing With The Stars*. I remember not wanting a relationship at the time but he was so charming and so much fun to be around. All of a sudden it hit me like a tonne of bricks and he was all I could think about. Thankfully he felt the same way.

EXPANDING THE FAMILY

Tristan and I enjoyed married life and four years together before even discussing the topic of children. I had just started a production company in LA with my friends (actors Rachael Taylor and Luke Baines) creating narrative content for brands, as well as writing my first feature film and a web series. We were living half the year in London, where Tristan was working on the UK version of the show, and the other half in Los Angeles. I was twenty-nine and I just had this overwhelming want to have a child. It didn't scare me that we were living this nomadic lifestyle and my work was all over the place. Unfortunately we had a miscarriage but by some miracle fell pregnant spontaneously with Echo a couple of weeks later.

It was quite honestly the best, most magical surprise I had ever experienced. Once I was pregnant, I continued to work. I directed a short film, was an assistant director on an Australian feature film, produced some commercial content and finished scripts. I was pregnant, not sick. Sure, there were a few occasions I had to throw up into a garbage bin on set or could barely keep my eyes open but I never let that stop me.

I wish there was an eloquent sentence that encapsulates the feeling I had when I met Echo for the first time. I was utterly besotted and completely in love.

'Happiness is a choice. I can actually choose to be happy and that is the most liberating feeling on earth.'

JUGGLING IT ALL

Echo was quite a good baby and by all accounts I had a healthy pregnancy and birth that I was up and about two days after. I didn't really ever stop working. So I just kept continuing what I was working on yet micro-managed my time with looking after a newborn and making sure she had my undivided attention when she needed me. I have always been a worker, it's part of my DNA so I guess it felt completely natural to me.

In terms of the juggle, I have good days and bad days. Days I feel I nail the motherhood/work balance and days I can barely manage to shower myself. I think what I have learned to respect is the nature of the uncertain, something I struggled with. I like a good plan and with a child you can try your best but generally the plan goes out the window. The best case scenario in my head is that Echo's needs are met first and I manage to accomplish one of my own goals during the day. If that means replying to an email, then so be it. I certainly try to be more efficient with my time and rely on my family and my wonderful husband to pick up the pieces that I may have missed. You just try your best. That's all you can do. Although I'm currently pregnant with our second, so I am sure I will have different response in about nine months time.

Everything has changed in the best possible way. Parenting is not easy and no doubt there will be days I am tested, but overall a sense of contentment floods me when I look at our daughter. I am certainly more gentle with myself but my intolerance for injustice and basic human nastiness is completely heightened. I look at the world through her eyes and try my best to make it a better place for her.

LESSONS FROM MY MUM

My mother taught me resilience and the ability to laugh at yourself even in the worst of circumstance. She is a great mother, the best. She is so completely selfless that it blows me away. If I could be half the mum she is I know I am doing a good job.

MUMMA ADVICE

I don't know if there is one that particularly piece of advice that I've been given that stands out. I can't remember who said it to me but 'say yes to help' is a good one.

LESSONS FOR MY DAUGHTER

If I could install kindness, humour and the ability to work for what she wants in life, then my work is done. I certainly don't want her to go through the trials and tribulations I had to endure but I know at some point she is going to have to learn things for herself.

THE NEW JUGGLE

Besides working on creating a new human life, I have just signed on to direct a film in Los Angeles (slated to begin shooting six weeks after the birth!). I also have a drama series in development in Australia and a documentary exploring the stigma associated with miscarriage titled *MOM The Misunderstanding Of Miscarriage*. And another little surprise is a chance to go on tour with *Mrs Brown's Boys D'Musical*, as a performer again. This genuinely feels like the right time to also start exploring that world again and it's exciting. My husband is the choreographer and we are looking at touring together to keep our family as a unit while all the madness is happening. I'm sure we will figure it out.

HAPPINESS IS . . .

A choice. There is no this + this = happiness. I recently discovered I can actually choose to be happy and that is the most liberating feeling on earth.

BIOLOGY IS THE LEAST OF WHAT MAKES SOMEONE A MOTHER.

OPRAH WINFREY

Photography: Alice Mahran

OLIVIA BOND

PRIVATE JEWELLER, GEMMOLOGIST, MUM OF TWO

'Being present with your children when you are with them is so important, otherwise it just all blurs into the same thing where you give neither your work nor your children your full attention.'

I grew up in Perth near the ocean, so there was a lot of time spent outdoors and at the beach. We would also spend long weekends and school holidays in Margaret River, where my sister and I would play in the bushland and down at the river catching tadpoles. It was idyllic and very Australian!

THE WORLD OF DIAMONDS

I moved to London straight after I finished university. Fairly soon after I arrived, I managed to secure a role at Sotheby's auction house on New Bond Street. Jobs there are highly coveted, and to this day I don't know how I managed to land one! I loved every moment. The standard of art and jewels that comes through those doors is just exceptional. Being able to work surrounded by works by Picasso or Modigliani was just an amazing experience. I remember I did an educational tour of a jewellery sale with Joanna Hardy, senior jewellery specialist at the time. As she discussed how the jewels have evolved over time and how they reflected the social and political climates of the era they were made, that's when I had my 'Aha!' moment. I then worked in Bvlgari in Sydney while also completing my Diploma in Gemmology, and completing Diamond Grading and Valuing courses. Through my job, I was able to build relationships with jewellers and wholesalers. When I became pregnant with my first daughter, I realised it would be better for me to start on my own and have more flexibility, so Olivia Bond Diamonds was born!

FINDING LOVE

Jeremy and I both grew up in the western suburbs of Perth where everyone knows everyone. Our paths crossed a few times before I accepted his invitation to go on a date. We always laugh about how I could never remember meeting him the first few times we ran into each other. He thought I was just trying to play it cool but I genuinely didn't remember him! For our first date, we went out for Japanese. We had so much fun drinking sake and talking for hours that we were the last people

'Pretty much the day after our first date I knew he was The One. I had never had a date like it before and I just knew this was it.'

left in the restaurant. The staff ended up giving us a bottle of dessert wine to take away so they could close up! I fell in love with his intelligence, his sense of fun and his enormous generosity. Pretty much the day after our first date I knew he was The One. I had never had a date like it before and I just knew this was it.

ENTERING MOTHERHOOD

I found becoming a mother for the first time completely overwhelming. It was the lifestyle adjustment that hit me the hardest. It's a difficult thing to fathom before you experience it yourself. I also put a lot of pressure on myself to try to continue on as I had pre-baby. It's a tall order and something I watch a lot of other new mums go through. Personally, it was when I accepted that life was simply different now and that I had to just go with the flow a bit more that I began to really enjoy being a mother.

THE JUGGLE

After my daughter Lulu's birth, I didn't even try to juggle anything at first. I just tried to keep my head above water and do my best as I learned about her and her needs. I really wanted to prioritise that in those first few months. When things settled down, I felt ready and I was able to be away from her a bit more (when I wasn't on call 24/7 as a milk buffet!). I began to accept more work again. The main challenge was often just finding the motivation to work when you have a small baby. I would find myself with emails to respond to and jobs to follow up but all I wanted to do was sit on the floor and play with my girls. Working from home a lot is wonderful because it provides flexibility, but it definitely means you need to be very disciplined about sitting down and working when you need to. On the flipside, being present with your children when you are with them is so important, otherwise it just all blurs into the same thing where you give neither your work nor your children your full attention.

MUM MOMENTS

I will say that now I have two babies, it takes an awful lot to make me embarrassed! These days a temper tantrum in the grocery store or an explosion from the nappy in a cafe just usually make me laugh! I have learned that motherhood is just even more challenging if you take it all too seriously.

MUM ADVICE

My mother has taught me (and continues to teach me) so much. From how to be selfless to how to cook, to remembering to always pack your bikini in your suitcase no matter where you are travelling! My advice for other mums is don't be afraid to ask for or accept help when it's offered. People like to help, it makes them feel good, and it doesn't mean you are not competent! And also, when it all gets too much, go back to basics and cross off everything that can wait from your to-do list. Sometimes you just need to keep life as simple as possible to get through. I call it 'survival mode'.

LESSONS FOR MY DAUGHTERS

I want to teach my daughters to always be kind, and not to rush to judgement. I also think it's important to instil in girls that is important to help raise each other up rather than cutting each other down.

THINGS THAT MAKE ME SMILE . . .

My girls all sleepy and cuddly when they first wake up in the morning. Finding amazing rare pieces of jewellery in antique stores and at auction (not necessarily to buy but to admire). Going to restaurants and eating delicious food with my wonderful husband.

Photograph: Alice

LISA WIPFLI

WIFE, MUM, CO-OWNER NOURISHING BUBS

'Motherhood is tiring, it's dirty, it's fun, it's emotional, it's selfless, it's physical, it's empowering, it's heartbreaking and it's truly wonderful and quite often all of these realities in one day.'

I had a very happy and humble family life living on the Gold Coast for primary school and Brisbane for high school. My parents both worked full-time to put my sister and me through private school, and we didn't want for anything. We spent so much time on the beach and out in the sunshine. We had a very happy, healthy and active childhood.

My teen years were a lot of fun. We lived in a home that had a separate retreat under the house with no internal access, so it was essentially like my own apartment at the age of fifteen. I had a separate bathroom, kitchen, lounge room and bedroom which my mum would clean every week (what a spoilt girl). I loved it and thought I was the coolest kid around. Looking back I realise I was a very lucky girl.

The love and selfless care I was given from my parents all my life has really made me the mother I am today. I'm so grateful for their love, support, guidance and the confidence they always had in me. I count myself lucky to have had the upbringing and family I had because, let's face it, the family you're born into really is the luck of the draw. I won big time.

CAREER PROGRESSION

I started in function planning and marketing for a restaurant and lounge bar in Brisbane. I then decided I wanted to work in advertising for a magazine or paper, so I got a job at the *Courier-Mail* in Brisbane. After a few years working there I moved to London working for *The Financial Times* and then I moved to the *Daily Mail* and *MailOnline*. After a four-year stint in London and a breakup that made me question where I wanted to live long term, I decided to move home to Australia. After the bustling life of London (which will always hold a very special place in my heart), I knew I couldn't move back to Brisbane, so I decided to give Sydney a shot. At first even Sydney seemed like a sleepy town, but I very quickly fell head over heels in love with it.

The highlight of my career has been when I told my boss at the *MailOnline* that I wanted to move home to Australia, she offered me an incredible opportunity to start scoping out the Australian market for us to begin monetising the Australian inventory. It was equally exciting and challenging. I underestimated how hard it would be pitching a British product to the Australian advertising agencies and while a lot of agency employees are English, it was still a difficult pitch. I was a one-woman show, with my boss in London, so I felt truly honoured to be given this trust and responsibility, and to be the first person in Australia to represent the brand.

EXPANDING THE FAMILY

I was working at a start-up digital business called VOLT Media as their sales director when I fell pregnant. Although we were a small business, it was the most fun and the warmest team I have been a part of. I was very lucky to be working for such an understanding new-age company with a great boss, who allowed me to work from home if I wasn't feeling well. I was still on maternity leave when I fell pregnant with my second child, Jack. Gosh that was a surprise – a wonderful surprise of course. Ted was only six months old, so after the initial shock subsided, we were overjoyed and I resigned from my job, as I knew it wasn't fair for a small business to hold my job for such a long period of time. I also made the decision that I didn't want to go back to work, and I wanted to give full-time parenting a red-hot go.

Meeting Ted was beyond words. It was the most emotional, overwhelming, happiest day of my life. Everything was a first and that's pretty special, because you don't have many days like that. The first time I gave birth, the first time I held my first child, the first time I breastfed.

I still get emotional when I think about this day and when I see photos. I would say that I wish I could relive it again, but I'm fortunate enough that my husband had a GoPro on his head, so we can relive it whenever we want. (Insert rolling eyes and grateful hands emoji.)

POSTNATAL DEPRESSION

Boy oh boy, two babies under two was a game changer for me. Ted and Jack are sixteen months apart in age and Jack was unfortunately a reflux baby, which added to the chaos of raising a newborn and a toddler. I thought I was absolutely killing it for the first five months of having two babies. I was getting them into a sleep routine, I was doing at least three loads of washing a day, I was cooking dinner, exercising, catching up with friends, doing the night feeds, ironing and I got to the stage where I felt like I couldn't sit still, I always wanted to be productive. It felt good, I was supermum . . . or so I thought. Until all of a sudden I realised when it came to bedtime I couldn't switch off. There was no off button for all of that energy, and I would lie awake at night buzzing … literally. I could hear a buzzing in my ears.

A lot of broken sleep at night due to night feeds turned into a lot of nights just lying awake unable to sleep. At my worst I was sleeping two to three hours a night. Then a number of other symptoms started kicking in, like loss of appetite, being overwhelmed by the smallest of tasks, always anxious with a knot in my stomach, experiencing quite a numb feeling, no motivation to exercise, no enthusiasm to do the usual activities with the kids. I Dr Googled myself with an underactive thyroid, however, after a thorough blood test, this came back all clear along with the rest of my bloods. Then to my surprise, and relief, I was finally diagnosed with postnatal depression and anxiety.

Since getting my PND situation under control through natural remedies and medication, I love being a mother of two children. I treasure every day with my boys and I've never laughed and loved so much in all my life.

THE JUGGLE

Oh the juggle is real. Sometimes, to be honest, I don't feel like I cope. If the kids are sick the juggle turns into all balls on the floor, but on a good week I cope by being organised. Keeping on top of the washing, meal planning, and staying focused at work with a detailed to-do list.

I think one of the highlights, or should I say lowlights, was when we all shared a dodgy sausage roll, care of my husband and his love of junk food. We were in Melbourne and I was the lucky one to be hit first with the food poisoning bullet, Ted was hit about 30 minutes after that, and then the next day, Jack and Mike (Wippa) went down. It was one of those nights when we ran out of sheets from all the vomiting and was topped off with Ted and me spending a night in hospital sharing one single bed in the foetal position as we hugged our buckets. Needless to say, not one of us has touched a sausage roll ever since.

RETURNING TO WORK

I was in a very fortunate position that after having Ted and Jack sixteen months apart, I didn't have the pressure to go back to a full-time job. I had resigned from my advertising role and was hungry to start using my brain again, so I was considering my next move. It's a really difficult decision for women and the strain of either having

$14
HUNTER
HUNTER

to go back to work because of financial reasons or because you feel societal pressure, can put a lot of unnecessary guilt on a women to be away from their children. While I did feel a bit of pressure from society, for me it was just about doing something that I was passionate about and having a project outside of raising my children. I started working on a couple of business ideas, but nothing that really put enough fire in my belly, then one day our babysitter, Olivia Bates, started telling me about a business that she was about to launch, a baby food business. Liv is also a Paediatric Nutritionist so I was excited to hear more.

NOURISHING BUBS

After seeing the packaging, learning about the product and researching the market, I decided I wanted to be involved in the business Nourishing Bubs, so I became Liv's business partner. I'm so fortunate that my role means I don't work full-time, and I fit in my work around the children's sleep times and a couple of daycare days. It's the perfect balance for me, so I have zero guilt and I feel so passionatel about Nourishing Bubs that it never feels like work.

Nourishing Bubs is a convenient and healthy baby food option for parents when they are first starting their baby on solids. The product we are best known for is our Starter Pack, which is a tray of forty cubes of snap frozen puree of ten different vegetables. The cubes are the right portion for an infant of four and a half to five months when it's time to start solids and there is absolutely nothing else added, no salt, water, preservatives or sugar, it's just 100 per cent vegetables. There are individual vegetables in each cube so parents can detect any allergies. As a baby's appetite begins to increase and texture needs to be added, you can simply build on these purees by mixing vegetables together, adding grains like quinoa or brown rice as well as protein. We are also about to launch some new products, which is very exciting.

SOCIAL MEDIA VS THE REALITY

When speaking about the realities of motherhood, one thing that comes to mind is do not, I repeat do not, use Instagram as a benchmark. Mums of Instagram are beautiful and amazing and desirable but it's not reality. They are just snapshots of gorgeous moments in a mother's life with her child. Look at these photos, like these photos, comment on these photos, but just know that after that mum took that photo of their child, the child probably had a tantrum and destroyed everything in close proximity or at the very least threw a toy at the mother's head. Motherhood is tiring, it's dirty, it's fun, it's emotional, it's selfless, it's physical, it's empowering, it's heartbreaking and it's truly wonderful and quite often all of these realities in one day.

What you see on my social media page is not what life is always like. I don't want to bore people with photos of me looking terrible in a bad tracksuit with no make-up on and when the house is a mess and the kids are sick. I definitely don't stage any photos, but usually the times when I'm more likely to take photos are when the kids are happy and healthy and I'm decently dressed.

To be honest, I love that Instagram is for people's happy, beautiful images. I don't find it depressing or compare my life to others. Of course I don't think it's right if people are staging photos or photoshopping their bodies but if it's just lovely snapshots of people's lives, then I'm okay with it. We just need to remember it's a light social platform and it needs to be used for escapism rather than a benchmark for success or comparison.

I WANT TO TEACH MY SONS . . .

To be polite, respectful, compassionate and strong boys. I want to teach Ted and Jack that being polite, respectful and compassionate doesn't make you weak. In fact, you are a stronger boy or man for having these values. I also want to teach them that if they work hard and are passionate they can achieve anything they want.

MOST IMPORTANT LESSON AS A MUM

Without doubt the most important lesson I've learned is that life can be full of superficial things (and people) and a lot of fluff (and boy did I used to get caught up in this), but now none of this matters and as long as my children are healthy and happy, life is complete.

LESSONS FROM MY MUM

Mum always said to me, 'Marry someone who makes you laugh,' and I'm so glad I listed to her. Mike/Wippa makes me laugh every single day and life is just more fun with him in it. She also taught me how to be the most selfless and caring mother and I like to think I'm doing a pretty good job at carrying on these values.

HAPPINESS IS . . .

Seeing my boys smile. As long as they are healthy and smiling, I'm the happiest I can be.

COMPANY

AMY DAWES

FOUNDER OF AUSTRALASIAN BIRTH TRAUMA ASSOCIATION, MOTHER OF TWO

'As a mother of daughters, I want to create a better future for them. Everyday I get to do that. We support women and their families impacted by a difficult birth experience. We also advocate for women in the hope that we will see maternity outcomes improve across Australia and the world.'

I spent a lot of time outdoors enjoying exercise, I'm a firm believer in exercising for body and mind. You name it I did it, from Muay Thai to yoga, dancing to AFL drills with my man. Weightlifting was my favourite. I was actually training for a fitness competition when I found out I was pregnant. I also have a huge thirst for learning so I spent a lot of time outside work studying courses in health and wellness. In 2011 I did my Certificate III and IV in fitness and became a qualified personal trainer for general interest. It's strange how the universe works as I always wanted to work with mums and now I do.

I was working as a business development manager for an award-winning restaurant in Sydney when I fell pregnant. Meeting my daughter for the first time was way too brief. She was taken out the room with my partner and it was a couple of hours before I saw her again. The first few days were a blur but I do remember thinking how calm she was, and in hindsight perhaps she knew she was born during a traumatic birth because she has been so easygoing.

BIRTH TRAUMA

Birth trauma is very individual; it could be psychological and/or physical trauma. It doesn't matter what kind of birth you have: vaginal, vaginal with intervention, emergency C-section, planned C-section or the birth of your dreams. No matter how straightforward it looks from the outside, you can still feel traumatised by it (equally, people can go through even the most complicated births and come out the other side okay). For me, my trauma was as a result of the injuries I sustained. I had a forceps delivery that resulted in a third degree perineal tear and pelvic floor muscle trauma. As a first-time mum, I had nothing to compare my experience to. Initially I didn't identify my birth as traumatic. Although I felt terrible, I was also grateful to have a healthy baby.

For five days I was bedridden with a catheter, finally wheeled outside in a wheelchair for fresh air on day six and home on day seven, with a pit stop at the chemist to pick up my many painkillers (a world away from the 'natural' birth I'd aspired to). My early days of motherhood were spent trying to find a comfortable way to sit, struggling to breastfeed and generally feeling not quite right. I always thought things would get better but instead at sixteen months postpartum I ended up prolapsing and the true extent of my birth injuries was discovered.

Shortly after diagnosis, I was suffering badly from anxiety and my amazing women's health physiotherapist recommended that I speak to a mental health professional. Here's the thing with birth injuries: because you can't see it, no one knows it's there, so no one knows just how much you're suffering. Yet having a prolapse has a serious impact over quality of life. It affects not just the mother but also everyone around her. I went from being fiercely independent and strong to feeling like I would never be the mother I thought I'd be, like I was old before my time. It's now been three years since my initial diagnosis and I'm in a much better place mentally. I've had to find other ways to keep active; it's been a slow process but I've developed a huge love for hiking.

STARTING THE BIRTH TRAUMA ASSOCIATION

When I was first diagnosed with severe pelvic floor muscle trauma, I remember arriving home from my physio appointment and googling physical birth trauma and nothing coming up. I'd never heard of prolapse and I'd never heard anyone else mention it so I thought I was the only one. I felt alone and I felt utterly broken. I then started researching and I soon discovered how common prolapse is; around 50 per cent of mothers will experience prolapse at some point in their lives. It made me wonder how many women there are suffering in silence! Through my research I discovered the work of my co-founders; Professor Hans Peter Dietz and his PhD student, midwife Elizabeth Skinner. I reached out to them because I strongly felt that I needed to be a voice, that I needed to speak out in the hope that I could help others.

When Elizabeth floated the idea of starting a birth trauma association in Australia with me, I thought to myself, 'I can make that happen.' It took a year to get our charity status, during which time I was pregnant with my second child. I was writing a business plan with a newborn on my lap! We finally launched in September 2017.

We support women and their families impacted by a difficult birth experience, while providing information to healthcare providers on how to better prevent, diagnose, treat and support. We also advocate for women in the hope that we will see maternity outcomes improve across Australia and the world.

My second birth was SO. MUCH. BETTER. I went private the second time, as I needed continuity of care. I also opted for an elective caesarean. One of the many misconceptions about caesareans is that the recovery time is long and hard, when in fact elective caesareans are very different from emergency caesareans. While it is major surgery with risks involved, I found it extremely cathartic to be out walking with my baby at only a week postpartum when it took me almost four weeks to walk properly after my first child.

HELPING OTHER WOMEN

Without a doubt the Australasian Birth Trauma Association (ABTA) has helped women realise that they aren't alone and that they don't need to suffer in silence. We launched only a year ago and we have around 600 members in our support group as well as providing peer support through live chat on our website. We are one of very few charities in the world raising awareness for psychological and physical birth trauma. We are breaking one of the last taboos around women's health.

MY WORLD

I have been most proud when I found out that I was pregnant with my first child, both friends and family struggled to imagine me as a mother! I couldn't imagine myself as a mother either. But it's without a doubt been my favourite job. I've surprised even myself. I am so proud to have my babies and I really strive to raise kids that care about the world around them.

Career-wise, I am definitely proud of what I'm doing now. ABTA has grown so much in just a year. Six months after we launched I secured funding for our first paid role and I was able to recruit our incredible volunteer manager to look after our peer support mentors, and further broaden our reach across Australia and New Zealand, and crucially provide more support to those that need it.

ADVICE TO OTHER MOTHERS

To prevent birth trauma, I strongly recommend approaching birth with an open mind, work out what is best for you and your body because a healthy baby needs a healthy mama. There is way too much focus on the

'perfect birth' when instead we need to shift the focus into the motherhood transition and better support women during recovery, and the huge shift we go through as we become mums. I also think finding a doula that supports a woman's right to choose, be it vaginal birth or caesarean would be great. Finding someone else to advocate for you and also to support your recovery. If you want a vaginal birth then you need to find a healthcare provider that will do their best to help you achieve that, by preparing you for labour and being honest about the risks involved. Surround yourself with people that provide a supportive decision-making approach.

For anyone who has been through a difficult birth experience, be gentle with yourself. Your body has done an amazing thing to give birth so do not feel ashamed if you are struggling to cope. Often, women and their families are so focused on the baby that the emotional wellbeing of the mother takes a lower priority. It is so important that you seek help for any symptoms you may be experiencing and if your feelings are dismissed, seek a second opinion. It's also important to acknowledge that partners or caregivers can also experience birth trauma and there is help and support available, you aren't alone.

HAPPINESS IS . . .

Being with my kids and being away from my kids (in equal measures!), drinking a nice cool glass of dry white wine on a warm day and being outdoors in nature!

JACINTA TYNAN

NEWS ANCHOR, AUTHOR, MOTHER OF TWO

'As much as I wanted to be a mother I was genuinely worried about how I'd cope. I was careering towards a life change, which I had been led to believe would suck the energy, identity and life-force out of me. Which is why I got such a lovely surprise when my baby was born and it was nothing like that.'

I'm the third of six kids – four girls and two boys. We came from good breeding stock, you could say – my dad was one of five, my mum one of six – so I always just assumed I would have children of my own one day. We grew up in The Sutherland Shire, known simply as 'The Shire', a quintessentially suburban enclave of southern Sydney with a menagerie of pets and a boat ramp at the end of the road. We would put on concerts which I wrote the scripts for and directed, giving myself a starring role, of course.

ENTERING JOURNALISM

I actually wanted to be an actress but when I mentioned that to my high school careers counsellor in Year 11 she talked me out of it, telling me acting wasn't a stable career. Because I was good at English she suggested I do journalism, which seemed like a good alternative. So I took myself off to study communications at Charles Sturt University in Bathurst.

I've now been a journalist for more than twenty-five years, working as a TV news and current affairs reporter and news presenter for the ABC, Seven and Sky News both in Australia and overseas. I have published four books, write a column for *Sunday Life* magazine and freelance as a writer. I like to write about my own life lessons, vulnerabilities and growth, which I've come to understand usually resonates with others who are going through similar things. I also produce and present a segment called 'Change Makers' on Sky News where I interview people making a positive difference in the world. It's my attempt to use the airwaves for good.

BECOMING A WORKING MUM

I worked right up until both babies were born – quite literally – going into labour with my first baby while on air. I called my mum in a break between news bulletins and asked, 'How do I know if I'm in labour?' Mum, who had six kids of her own so she oughta know, told me if the contractions are 'regular' then I'm probably in labour. So I started timing them and recording it on my news script.

'When our eyes met for the first time, I was totally overwhelmed with a feeling of 'rightness'. I could no longer imagine a life without him.'

They were regular, all right. And they lasted for 48 more hours! After all that, my beautiful boy, Jasper, was born via emergency caesarean. I delivered my second son, Otis, naturally – called a V-BAC (vaginal birth after caesar) – nineteen months later. V-BACs aren't very common because most women think it's not possible but I'm here to tell you it is.

With my first birth, even in my post-caesarian drugged stupor, when my baby was handed to me over the surgical divide and placed on my chest, I was lucid enough to understand that this was a life-altering moment for both of us. It was love at an intensity I never knew was possible. When our eyes met for the first time, I was totally overwhelmed with a feeling of 'rightness'. I could no longer imagine a life without him in it, this little creature I had known for mere minutes. 'I love you already,' I whispered to him, 'Thank you for choosing me.'

THE UPSIDE OF MOTHERHOOD

From the minute I shared the news of my pregnancy, and well before that, really, I was bombarded with negative press about motherhood. 'It's the hardest job in the world,' people would say. 'Kiss goodbye to your life' was another common refrain. And 'You'll never sleep again.' It's the drudgery, the over-tiredness, the monotony that mothers talk about most. It sounded like a thankless task. As much as I wanted to be a mother, I was genuinely worried about how I'd cope. I was careering towards a life change, which I had been led to believe would suck the energy, identity and life-force out of me. For the rest of my life. With no turning back. Which is why I got such a lovely surprise when my baby was born and it was nothing like that. Awash with happiness and powered by the deepest love I'd ever known, I had never felt so content. I'd been told if you can get through the first six weeks with a new baby then you can get through anything. Yet these had been the happiest six weeks – and beyond – of my life. I was sleep deprived, sure – what new mother isn't? – and didn't have a second to myself and I had no idea what I was doing, but I was so at peace. So I decided to write about it. I wanted to describe the upside of motherhood, the joy and privilege of it. I didn't assume I had any superior knowledge or luck. I only had one baby at this point, a healthy one, and he wasn't even walking yet. But I did think that if I of all people could turn things around from the fear and trepidation I had felt about becoming a mother to quite enjoying myself, then it was worth sharing. I thought it might inspire other mothers to look at it a different way. The prevailing message of our time, the line we're all buying, is that motherhood is tough going. I wanted to question that manifesto.

My intention was to spread the love and I never anticipated it would cause such a stir. But I had unwittingly betrayed the unwritten motherhood code of uniting in our shared struggle. There were many comments from mothers grateful for my 'unique' positive perspective – thanking me for my 'bravery' in speaking up. But these were drowned out by the chorus of dissent from mothers who felt like I was judging them for having a different experience. The story went viral and the comments – many vicious and personal – went on for months, and it hurt. But I don't regret writing it because it sparked a conversation that was crying out to be had. I think it's time to question our approach to motherhood and find ways to make it less taxing, less isolating and more fulfilling. I came to see that, aside from women with postnatal depression or other mental illness, this attitude is rarely circumstantial. It's a choice.

MOTHER ZEN

After the dust eventually settled on my contentious 'motherhood is easy' story, (as it became known), it was clear that mothers were craving advice and support on how to make parenting more rewarding and even joyful. So I decided to write a book and start a website sharing information and insights that I was picking up along the way. The name 'Mother Zen' came to me in a meditation. I don't claim to be a zen mother (I wish!) but I'm aspiring to be. I desperately want to be more present and connected with my kids as I know this serves them and me.

STARTING AGAIN

Leaving home with my two young boys (when they were six and four) was one of the toughest decisions I've ever

made but I feel proud of myself for having the courage to follow through to give them the best chance of a happy and harmonious life. I'm also incredibly lucky that I had the resources to move out and start again which so many women don't have.

Being a single mum means being constantly on the case. I feel the need to be all things for my boys. I'm mindful of trying to find a way to merge my ingrained nurturing feminine energy – encouraging them to share their emotions and feelings – with the more masculine energy of creating boundaries and being firm on them where necessary. It also means playing 'garbage trucks' and kicking a ball with them even when I don't feel like it.

With my boys, I'm hyper alert to raising them to recognise inequality and foster empathy and compassion, for themselves and others. I feel the weight of responsibility for my sons' emotional wellbeing, and I encourage them to deal with 'bad feelings' as they come up – to establish this habit early – so it doesn't manifest as sadness and anger down the track. To make good men of them. My oldest boy, Jasper calls me the 'Worry ATM' as I get them to deposit their worries on my shoulders. I want them to know that I have their back, to carry surety of their mother's love with them throughout their lives.

I meditate – twice a day – which helps enormously. It keeps me focused, present and sane, and it fortifies me for when the wheels fall off. It is the thing.

The challenge with mothering young children, I find, is to constantly remember to watch ourselves as they observe us more than they listen. They take their cues from us and model our behaviour. I'm conscious of the life-defining decisions our kids are making about themselves and the world in every moment. I see it as my role to guide my boys to interpret things in a constructive way. At the same time I'm well aware that our kids teach us just as much as we teach them. Children are the best therapy. We're accountable to these little people who are looking to us for for guidance on how to be in the world. As parents we're called on to evolve, to be better. In the way we choose to treat our kids, we have the opportunity to heal ourselves.

I sometimes ask myself, 'How do I want my boys to remember me?' It always snaps me back into self-awareness, which benefits them too. I have a vested interest in being present – being aware of moments as they unfold – so I don't miss them and to mitigate potential regret as my boys grow up. It's a big ask but I try to remember to tune into them, to listen to them and validate them, to treat them with respect and apologise when I don't. And to draw boundaries which, they may not realise now, are for their own good. As mothers we have to surrender – to the chaos, the mess, the spontaneity.

I want to *know* my boys, not tell them who to be. I try to ask questions rather than dictate. I remind my boys that they're important, that they're here for a reason. 'Remember who you are,' I say to them. I believe that children only 'play up' when they're seeking connection and reassurance. It's up to me to gently offer that, while also being clear with what's appropriate and respectful of others. When I'm out of my depth, which I so often am, I usually ask myself 'What would love do now?' The solution can be found there. I'm no Mother Zen but I'm working on it.

I like myself so much more since I became a mother. It was such a relief to not have to think about myself anymore. I embrace the choicelessness of being required to be here right now. Of being needed. Being accountable to two little people has compelled me to step up, conscious that they're looking to me for guidance. I'm more present, for starters. I'm happier because I'm in a constant state of love. I'm kinder and more patient. I'm gentler. And when I lose it, as I too often do, I own it. Motherhood is just what I needed to bring me back into alignment with what matters. There's simply no time for anything else.

RETURNING TO WORK

When my boys were about nine months old, I went back to work two days a week presenting news, and I would write while they slept. I planned to take six months off work but I couldn't bear to leave them when the time came. These days I work at night two nights a week presenting news, which allows me to be with my boys during the day. I do my writing and other work when they're at school. I'm so grateful that I've been able to carve out a career that still allows me to be there for my children most of the time.

MUM ADVICE

Tune into your intuition. You know what you're doing. We're so often clouded by the voices of others when it comes to parenting, a cavalcade of unsolicited (often)

advice on what we should do, and it's easy to lose sight of our own truth. Ask yourself the question – as I often do – 'what does my child need from me right now?' It might seem counterintuitive in a world that tells us we're in charge, but it will bring you to the answer. And meditate. It helps you cope with anything.

MUM MOMENTS

If we can remember to find the humour in any situation, it helps ease the tension. I took my boys to the US when they were six and eight to ride The Polar Express in Flagstaff, Arizona. We also went to The Grand Canyon and Disneyland. It was a challenge driving on the 'wrong' side of the road, the only grownup in the car. There were stressful moments, like when we got lost on an LA freeway with two fractious kids in the back, but they were far outweighed by the thrill of this once-in-a-lifetime experience.

There have been many challenging times since leaving home with my boys, as they struggle to adapt to our change in circumstances. I see it as my role to pare it all back to basics, trying to determine what will matter most in the scheme of their lives. Like shared meals and shared moments. I go around the dinner table and say, 'Tell me the best bits of your day'. I read to them at bedtime no matter what, and I crawl into bed with each of them – their 'special time' – to offload and connect. It's my time too, to make up for things. For the times I wasn't present or lost my cool. In doing this my hope is that I'm teaching them about unconditional love (my eldest calls is 'UC'). And that tomorrow is a new day.

THREE THINGS THAT MAKE ME HAPPY . . .

My boys, of course. Meditation. I couldn't get by without it. Skiing on a good powder day.

'Tune into your intuition. You know what you are doing.'

BEING A MOTHER IS PROBABLY THE HARDEST JOB IN THE WORLD. CHILDREN COME INTO THE WORLD TO TEACH US.

MARIAH CAREY

KIRSTEN KING

FOUNDER OF FLUIDFORM PILATES, MOTHER OF THREE

'To hold your baby in your arms is one of the most precious experiences you can imagine. I looked at this special little human that we had created in total amazement, it truly is a miracle.'

A couple of years ago, I hurt my knee running and needed some rehab, plus some leaned-out thigh muscles in order to recuperate, so I started doing Pilates. I started in a studio that taught all of the Victorian Ballet students. Their movement and posture was so beautiful that I was hooked from the get-go.

CREATING FLUIDFORM PILATES

My clients came through word of mouth initially, and more recently Instagram. I have been very fortunate that clients talk about my studio and due to their positive experience, the talk has continued!

EXPANDING THE FAMILY

My birth with Charlie was so fast I was in shock for about two hours. Once I came around, I couldn't believe that she was mine. To hold your baby in your arms is one of the most precious experiences you can have. I continually felt myself looking in total amazement at this special little human we had created. It truly is a miracle. The biggest challenge after giving birth was the initial journey out into public. Learning that it was okay for your baby to cry and trusting that you could settle her. The whole breastfeeding thing in public terrified me too. But by baby number three (Harper) I could teach a class and breastfeed at the same time!

THE JUGGLE

My life now with three children is definitely busier and crazier, and I have had to learn to relax and go with the flow a little more. Becoming a mum has also made me more emotional, for the better. Running your own business that you are very much an integral part of on a daily basis proves very difficult when the topic of maternity leave comes up. We were relocating back to Sydney when we had Charlie (she was born in England) so it was a bit stop–start . But with Willow I came back to work at eleven weeks, and nine weeks after Harper was born. At times I felt like I was missing out, but I have had

'Your children should become part of your lives, not you a part of theirs.'

to find the balance between being a great mum and great businesswoman. We don't have grandparents in Sydney so the responsibility of juggling a new baby meant we would go everywhere together, including work. You could say Willow and Harper grew up in the studio. They had their own cot and routine, and I managed my clients and classes around them. A few times I have totally lost the plot, but mostly I like to think I have had it under control. I worked out a routine that worked for me. I would do two hours of emails every night from two till four in the morning. This was usually when my babies would feed and because I was already awake, I would get loads of admin work done before having a power nap, then finally start the day. I am lucky I can survive on very little sleep. I always get organised for my day ahead the night before. Laying clothes out for both my girls and me, packing bags, etc. I had to be organised and feel in control otherwise I would never have been able to survive. Obviously the work–life balance has been difficult and a constant juggle, but with three young children, the balance between wife and mum has also been difficult. Layer this with running your own studios and it becomes very challenging. My staff has been integral in my success, but knowing who to employ, who is a good fit and what I actually needed took some time. I feel like I am in a great place with my employment strategy and my staff now.

HEALTH AND WELLBEING

I believe in everything in moderation. I am not a believer in depriving yourself of anything. Enjoy your life and put your health and wellbeing first but still have fun and treat yourself. In regards to your diet, have more good days than you have bad. When it comes to getting into exercise following having a baby, I always suggest to wait till you get the sign-off from your doctor. This happens at around the six-week mark. Some clients are desperate to start sooner, so as long as their body is feeling back to normal and they have done Pilates with me during their pregnancy, I am happy for them to return. We have a very structured and detailed program for returning mums.

ROLE MODELS

My role models are my mum and dad. Both have an unbelievable work ethic, but they were always still a strong presence in our lives. They have values and qualities that I hope people see and admire in me like I do in them. My mother always taught me to be patient and kind, and I try to live like that every day.

MOTHER ADVICE

The best advice I have ever been given as a mother is to make sure your children become part of your lives not you a part of theirs. And always trust your gut!

THINGS THAT MAKE ME SMILE ARE . . .

Seeing my girls run screaming to the front door when my husband Kingy comes home. And hearing my girls laugh.

LA PORTE

LA PORT

DAINA LINDSAY

FOUNDER OF PONO PROBIOTICS, MOTHER OF TWO

'It was astonishing how in a moment all the pain and exhaustion evaporated. No words can fully describe the feeling you experience when you meet your little one for the first time.'

I look back at my life before kids and it feels like I was in a parallel universe. I lived a 'work hard, play hard' lifestyle. I worked at a radio station in the advertising sales team – it was a high-pressure role with a fantastic group of people. It was very social with many events to attend throughout the week, lots of perks and the obligatory Friday night drinks. I was living a social single lifestyle, and found my work–life balance tiring but addictive. It was in August 2011 when I met my husband Dan on a Bali trip. Looking back at that time, it is amazing to think that he would one day become my husband. We clicked and realised we had a lot in common, and together began to slow down and plan a future.

OUR LITTLE FAMILY

Meeting Maija was a dream come true. One of the most magical days of my life. When she was born I felt an overwhelming feeling of contentment. I was a mum to a beautiful little girl, with Dan by my side. Life was perfect, she was perfect, and I was so proud of her. It was astonishing how in a moment all the pain and exhaustion evaporated and it was like bursting through clouds. There are no words that can fully describe the feeling you experience when you meet you little one for the first time. Sands was a beautiful, big boy. He was delivered naturally weighing a whopping 4.7 kilos. I certainly did not expect to deliver a three-month-old sized baby. He went straight into size 000 clothing. But, he was just divine. So handsome and I was so happy to have a boy. We took a while to name him. Because of his size the two names we had chosen just did not suit him. After nearly thirty-six hours we agreed on Sands, a name that runs in Dan's family. I could not imagine him being called anything else. He's our little Sandman!

Sands was always a happy, healthy boy. He was an easy baby, he fed well, slept well and I never had any problems. It wasn't until we moved to Brisbane, when he was 11 months old, that he started to experience repeated ear infections, hand foot and mouth, conjunctivitis, and almost every other illness under the sun. It was a very challenging two months. As a result of our relocation from South Australia to Queensland, we introduced the kids to a new childcare, new climate and new illnesses. After a few months of settling in and the kids catching everything, Sands ended up in intensive care with a respiratory infection. Following a twenty-four-hour stay in hospital, I began to look at the possibility that there may be a further underlying issue with his immune system. A very caring doctor explained the impact that antibiotics could have on gut flora and inspired me to begin a journey of research and learning into the importance of gut health for the entire family. This is what lead me to the creation of PONO Probiotics.

CREATING PONO PROBIOTICS

The aim was to create a product that could be seamlessly introduced into our daily routine. Kids are always very cautious when it comes to taking medicine, so my husband and I wanted to create something that wasn't medicinal. We wanted to produce industry-leading products in an approachable, tasty, family-friendly format. Dan and I were married in Hawaii, so when we discovered the ancient Hawaiian word *pono*, which means rightness, correctness, alignment, goodness, excellence and wellbeing, our choice was made. These are things that we hope for in life for ourselves, our families and also our health!

It was a funny day leaving my radio family and starting a journey on my own. We had reached a point where I was unable to stay on top of both roles and I was stretched too thin. I still stay in regular contact with many of the amazing people I worked with and they continue to be an amazing source of support and strength. I think when you are so passionate about something, and can live and breathe your brand, good things will happen. You never know what life will throw at you and it is so important to have great people around you. I have loved helping others embark on their own business journeys along the way too! Dan has not had a sick day in the last two years and the kids have not been sick enough to even consider antibiotics since we began our business journey.

THE JUGGLE

The juggle is *so* real. Honestly the juggle is a struggle, but I wouldn't have it any other way. I love my life and the flexibility I have. It's a lifestyle I created because I wanted it. I love that I am available to do drop-offs and pick-ups with my kids. It's a special time that I cherish. Mind you, right now is probably the hardest I have ever worked in my life. I cram as much work in as I can while the kids are at school and daycare, and then when the kids are at home I want to just be a mum and be present, giving them my full attention. Once the kids are tucked up in bed, I can jump back online and do what I need to do. What really works for me is to just take each day as it comes. I make a list that morning of what needs to be achieved and I try not to get too far ahead of myself. Sometimes, just thinking about what needs to be done long term can really overwhelm me, I try to just tackle each day. I find this eases my stress levels and any risk of anxiety.

Since having kids, I have certainly become more patient! I lack patience at the best of times, but that's one thing you really have to learn being a mum. Just breathe! If your toddler wants to go for a walk and smell every flower along the way, while you know you have 100 emails to get back to, you just embrace it and enjoy that moment. Your little ones grow up so quickly, so try to never rush things and soak up the special moments. It has also taught me to stop and take photos along the way. They are such a powerful way to reflect. I find myself looking back at our journey every few months and it blows my mind how quickly life moves, and reminds me how important it is to keep striving forwards.

MUM MOMENTS

One that comes to mind was my fifth day being a mum. I had been staying in a hotel for the last two nights (it's a fabulous program the hotel has with the hospital to make space for beds). Dan and I were walking out the entrance to get our car from the valet service, feeling ever so fancy with my brand-new daughter in my sparkling new pram. I just remember feeling so excited to get Maija home. Dan opened the car door and I went to click Maija's capsule out of the pram. I pressed the wrong release button and Maija in her capsule flew forward. Lucky she was strapped in tightly. I managed to grab the capsule just before it crashed to the concrete and calmly composed myself and clicked her into the car. I still cringe thinking what the concierge and valet staff thought of us.

LESSONS FROM MY MOTHER

My mother taught me so much growing up, however, it wasn't until her final months battling pancreatic

HANALEI
BAE

cancer that I learned the most. Her bravery and strength in the face of adversity was heroic. Mum taught me to roll up my sleeves and get things done.

The advice I'd give to other mums is to focus on you and your family, and do whatever works best for your little tribe. Don't try to compare your parenting to others. We are all so unique and what works for one will not necessarily work for another.

THINGS THAT MAKE ME HAPPY . . .

Running – I absolutely love the feeling. I call it my mediation! If I have not gone for a run in a few days I can feel my stress levels building in my shoulders, so I run four to five times a week. This keeps me feeling relaxed and happy! I love music and I have no real preference, I love all types. I just feel music lifts me up and can really enhance your mood. And of course my family (Dan and the kids) makes me happy. I can walk in the door all wound up after the most challenging day and all it takes is a funny comment, and a high five from my three-year-old to make me realise that family is number one and everything else is just a speedbump.

'Focus on you and your family, and whatever works best for your little tribe.'

HARMONY MOLTONI

DIRECTOR OF HARMONY & LAWSON, MUM

'It is definitely a difficult transition from being totally focused on yourself and work, to caring for a child 24/7. I think any modern, independent woman will tell you that.'

I grew up in Perth in Western Australia. Perth has a very active, outdoor lifestyle. We went boating a lot on the Swan River and to Rottnest Island, as well as to the country quite often. We also travelled overseas frequently. Perth is very isolated so my parents liked to get away to Europe, Asia and America as much as we could.

I was at university and really not enjoying my postgraduate course. I had learned about manufacturing, wholesaling and retailing working in Sydney, and decided to try my hand at producing something myself. It was basically a snowball effect from the first sample I made of my own clothing line; friends, their friends and relatives all wanted to buy what I was making. I knew at that point very early on that stores would also be interested. I made appointments around Australia in Brisbane, Gold Coast, Perth, Sydney and Melbourne to sell a small collection of clothing under the label Harmony & Lawson, Lawson being my brother's name. I quickly gained the support of Australia's leading retailers and the range grew to thirty-five styles and more than sixty colours. The children and home lines were established a few years later.

The biggest highlight of my career has been seeing Harmony & Lawson on the shelves and in the showrooms of leading retailers like Space Furniture, Top 3 By Design, Domo Furniture, Camerich Furniture, Green With Envy, Tuchuzy, Bessie Head and other leading retailers around Australia. Likewise, working with industry leaders like acclaimed interior designer Greg Natale.

GROWING THE FAMILY

Meeting my baby for the first time was surreal. You think about the moment for nine months and then when it happens it's almost a dream-like moment. I think in

'Don't be too hard on yourself and run your own race, don't compare yourself to other women. Make sure your take time out for yourself.'

dealing with the juggle, you establish a new normal, which is basically chaos for the first few months. Writing emails while breastfeeding, working while the baby sleeps and doing what I could around my responsibilities to Oscar was basically how the first few months unfolded.

My most embarrassing mum moment recently has been when my son yelled out on a flight recently, 'Mummy, my penis is talking to me! (Which is how I taught him to describe the sensation of having to go to the toilet.) I was a little bit embarrassed!

It is definitely a difficult transition from being totally focused on yourself and work, to caring for a child 24/7. I think any modern, independent woman will tell you that. Especially now as educated, Western women are empowered with a plethora of options in life. The biggest challenge for me was the sleep deprivation. Oscar was a very predictable, easy baby but he still woke during the night for the first twelve months. I now prioritise my time and have scaled back wholesaling in the last few years. No amount of money is worth missing out on your child's early years.

MUM ADVICE

Don't be too hard on yourself and run your own race; don't compare yourself to other women. Also, make sure you take time out for yourself. And be careful who you take advice from as everyone has an opinion. My mother taught me to always see the positive in everything and to really value your education.

LESSONS FOR MY CHILDREN

I want to teach them to work hard, be honest, treat people with respect and not to worry what anyone thinks of you.

THINGS THAT MAKE ME SMILE

My son's sense of humour, catching up with good friends and when my husband gets excited by something.

HAPPINESS IS ...

Being content with your life and enjoying the relationships of family and friends.

WHEN YOU ARE A MOTHER, YOU ARE NEVER REALLY ALONE IN YOUR THOUGHTS. A MOTHER ALWAYS HAS TO THINK TWICE, ONCE FOR HERSELF AND ONCE FOR HER CHILD.

SOPHIA LOREN

Photos supplied by ABC.

FATMA ELZEIN

FOUNDER OF MUMMIES PAYING IT FORWARD, MOTHER

'Motherhood has refocused my view on life and how I see the world.'

Growing up the youngest of four kids made for a fun and loud childhood! My memories of growing up were essentially really happy ones. We had a large extended family so there were always cousins to play with or people popping over. Having two older brothers and mainly boy cousins the same age as me, meant that I lived and breathed rugby league from a very early age and was taught how to properly tackle someone, which was always funny when we played a game because most of the boys never expected the 'girl' to take them out, but they learned quickly enough!

With my parents, although in a sense they both fulfilled very traditional roles having being born and raised in Lebanon in the 1950s and 60s, they understood how different our upbringing would be and ensured we saw how fortunate we were to grow up in a country like Australia and have the opportunities we had before us. Reflecting back on my childhood and in particular the years I had with my dad, who passed away close to seventeen years ago now, the greatest gift I received from my parents was the feeling of being loved unconditionally and protected, and that no matter what, they were there for us and wanted the best for us. The gift of being loved unconditionally and the faith my father had in me even before I really believed in myself was so profound. It not only sustained the years of my childhood but it has also been a great comfort in the years since his sudden passing. I think his impact on my life continues to this very day, especially since becoming a mother and navigating through the complexities of parenthood.

GIVING BACK

Talking about why I founded Mummies Paying It Forward remains so difficult for me to this very day. The idea for this charity came from what was the most difficult, devastating and profound period of my life. For so many years, I'd lived with a false sense of security and a strongly held belief that I could protect those that I loved, but sometimes life shows us that, irrespective of how deep your love is for someone, what you know or the skills you've developed throughout your career in caring for others, sometimes life is unfair and the child you'd hoped to have a long and happy life and who you believed would outlive you, and who'd brought your family so much joy on her birth, would be taken suddenly. That kind of loss is so profound that your view on your whole existence is shattered beyond comprehension and you start to doubt everything you've ever known.

Life is forever split in two parts, before and after. The

interesting thing about grief is it can break you to a point that you lose faith in yourself, you lose the ability to see that the present day is just that, a gift that we often take for granted. But grief can also motivate you to do and achieve far more than was ever imagined conceivable.

Your motivation to find meaning and a purpose within your grief isn't from a spreadsheet or a report but from the limitless depth of your heart and soul.

Prior to Mummies Paying It Forward, life consisted of the organised chaos that comes with raising four young children and working part time as a paediatric nurse. It was a juggle especially after the twins came along. Going from one child to two, as most mums would understand, was challenging. But going from two children to four was a showstopper. Focusing wholeheartedly on supporting our expanding family unit was the number one priority at the time. As the children got a little older, returning to work as a paediatric nurse was very important to me. Nursing sick children and their families is a great passion of mine and although juggling the two roles was stressful and exhausting at times, continuing to dedicate a part of my life to nursing was and continues to be extremely important.

THE CHARITY

Mummies Paying It Forward is a Sydney-based charity created to support the most vulnerable people within our society, by providing pre-loved and brand new items to a wide range of dedicated local not-for-profit charities in NSW. We have helped women in refuges, families in need within the community, refugee families, the homeless and more. Although we do focus heavily on supporting mums and bubs, the main objective for Mummies Paying It Forward is to provide support in the form of material donations to where it's needed the most. The objective is to support those in need irrespective of race, religion, gender, age or sexual orientation. For donors, it is about knowing that their donations in good or great condition, which at times hold sentimental value, will be distributed to individuals and families in need – rather than resold.

MOTHERHOOD

Motherhood has refocused my view on life and how I see the world. For a large part, life before kids was very much egocentric but becoming a mum changed the focus from me to them and also the world we live in. While you become more passionate and driven about the community and society in general, motherhood can also make you feel more vulnerable. You want to protect your kids from life's struggles, but as they get older you know that they need to experience life for themselves to become independent individuals and develop resilience to what life throws at them. While it's the most challenging role I've ever faced, it's also rewarding and joyful, especially when they've all gone to bed!

THE JUGGLE

Most days feel like a race to try to fit it all in but for me it's about recognising what's important and prioritising what needs to be done on each given day. I've learned to let go of a lot and prioritise time for myself each day, and that comes in the form of reading. My Kindle is my most beloved possession and having that time, even if it's just ten or fifteen minutes at the end of the night to lose yourself in a book, is a great way to tune out from life. As mums we become really good at giving ourselves to our children, families, friends, to our jobs and things we are passionate about, but it's important to also focus on you.

Juggling it all sometimes sounds like we're on top of everything and I don't believe we really can be. I probably am never going to catch up with the seemingly endless loads of washing my family produces, or manage to exercise as much as I should as well as spend time with the kids, work, volunteer and also have time for my partner and myself. But prioritising what needs my time and focus on any given day is important to do. I often have my phone on silent when the kids are around so I don't get distracted. Once they're tucked up in bed, that's when I can focus on what else I have to do.

VALUES I HOPE TO TEACH MY CHILDREN . . .

Respect. Compassion. Empathy. Resilience. Gratitude.

MUMMIES PAYING IT FORWARD

A Sydney charity providing donations of new and pre-loved baby and children's clothes, books, toiletries and non-perishable food to families in need. Visit **mummiespayingitforward.org.au** to find your nearest drop-off point.

Photos supplied by ABC

Photos supplied by ABC

SOPHIE VAN DEN AKKER

CO-FOUNDER OF VAULT ACTIVE, AUSTRALIAN MODEL, MOTHER OF TWO

'Becoming a mum was a feeling that still now brings tears to my eyes – the feeling of those first few seconds was a mixture of utter shock and instant love.'

I am the baby of five kids, so there was always plenty happening. I loved to dance and sing, but my favourite thing to do was spend time with Mum. My childhood is a happy memory.

STARTING A BUSINESS

When making that incredibly scary decision to start a new venture and head into the unknown to create what was always a dream of mine, it was my lifelong best friend standing right next to me who encouraged me to press forward and said, 'Buckle up, we're about to do this!' That really helped me. Creating my activewear line Vault Active was something that came naturally as we were so passionate about the health and fitness industry. We could never find exactly what we were looking for, which motivated us every day to do something new. But we didn't want this to just represent a normal activewear brand. Instead we set out with a goal to inspire and motivate women all over the world.

AUSTRALIA'S NEXT TOP MODEL

Being on *Australia's Next Top Model* was the biggest learning curve for me as a model. It threw me in the deep end and challenged me every single day. I learned to deal with different emotions and personalities as well as gain an idea of what the modelling industry was all about. The show put me on a platform that I will always be grateful for, providing me with opportunities that have lead me to my success to date.

One of the highlights of my career definitely would have been when I became the face of Melbourne Spring Fashion Week. Being the face of MSFW was the launch pad for me to become an international model. Doors opened to opportunities that I never knew were possible and for that I am eternally grateful to the city of Melbourne.

THE CHALLENGES

There have been many challenges in my life, whether they have been personal or professional, like learning a new business, making adjustments to motherhood, dealing with new situations or having the pressure of studying. The most important thing to me has been that I am continuing to learn and grow from these challenges. This has allowed me to be more prepared, to stay positive and have a plan B in place.

BECOMING A MUM

Becoming a mum was a feeling that still now brings tears to my eyes – the feeling of those first few seconds was a mixture of utter shock and instant love. It has been such a long journey to get to this moment with so many overwhelming thoughts. It was the moment in life for me where time slowed down and everything became quiet

'Do the best you can, thrive to be happy and do what is going to work for you and your family.'

and clear. My entire world has shifted since giving birth. Suddenly what I thought was so important wasn't anymore! Having a child really puts life into perspective and gets your priorities in line. There were many adjustments I was yet to learn and find myself continuing to learn. Friendship circles change too. I now can't wait for bedtime and I am finding I live a much healthier lifestyle. I found a new respect for my parents and understand now why they put themselves last.

JUGGLING MOTHERHOOD AND CAREER

I juggle motherhood and my career with difficulty! Multitasking really is the key. I know us women say this all the time but it's the truth! I find myself some days holding my daughter Layla while on a conference call and tidying up at the same time. Anyone with a toddler knows the little tornadoes are constant. I absolutely love what I do, and for me it's about time management, thinking outside the box and setting a good example.

HEALTH AND WELLNESS

Physical, emotional and spiritual health and wellbeing play such a huge role in my life. I always keep in the back of my mind what it is that I need to be doing to feel amazing, stay on track and to be a good role model for my children. I believe that eating healthily sets a good example for my children. I make exercise a priority and ensure we all have those time-outs to reset and debrief. I always like to sit down and simply talk. It's really difficult now to just relax in life with so much happening around the world. Those time-outs are important to get centered and continue on a positive path.

THINGS THAT MAKE ME SMILE

My daughter, dancing and getting together with friends who I haven't seen in a while.

MY PROUDEST ACHIEVEMENT

Becoming a mother, nothing in the world could have prepared me for what was to come and still is coming. Easily the proudest moment in my life.

Success to me is being happy. It means creating a business that empowers the community, being in a position to help others and lead everyone, together, to a happier and healthier life!

MY ROLE MODEL IS . . .

My mother Carmen Van Den Akker. She is such a strong woman with high values, integrity and such selflessness. A woman I could only dream of being half of. The woman who has taught me so much to be myself, be confident and always be kind.

She taught me to always be content and happy with what I have, to be myself and to not compare myself to others. To be kind and help where possible and to continue to grow; grow as her daughter, grow as a mother, a friend, a colleague and to be passionate in all I do!

BEST ADVICE GIVEN AS A MOTHER

The best advice I've been given is to do the best I can, thrive to be happy, to not doubt myself and do what is going to work for me and my family.

HAPPINESS IS . . .

Being in that moment of utter peace surrounded by loved ones, smiling and laughing at the stupid things in life.

V.A

V.A

KRISTIN RAWSON

INTERIOR AND GLOBAL FASHION STYLIST, MOTHER

'Let go of the small things – a tidy house or a pile of washing doesn't really matter. What matters is spending that time focused on your children's needs. Let go of whatever you need to sleep, rest and restore to enable you to do it all again the next day.'

I had a very happy and fulfilled childhood, based on the Northern Beaches of Sydney with three siblings. I have fond memories of a balanced household, school, co-curricular activities and lots of outdoor play with friends and family. Australia is an amazing place to grow up. I am grateful to have had nearly a decade in New York in my twenties now to be back in Australia raising my children here.

A PASSION FOR FASHION

During high school I did work experience with one of Australia's greatest fashion stylists, Nicole Bonython-Hines. The on-set experience and being taught all the tricks of the trade was essential for setting me up to work overseas. I was able to work across magazines like *Harpers Bazaar* and *Teen Vogue* in New York, which were amazing experiences. I lived in New York most of my twenties assisting one of the industry's greatest fashion sylists (who is also Australian), Brana Wolf. She was at the time the Fashion Director of *Harper's Bazaar.* We spent our time shooting for the magazine and consulting for global fashion designers in New York, London, Milan and Paris, attending the fashion weeks around the world during fashion month twice a year. The highlights including Donatella at Versace and Michael Kors in New York to name a few!

Brana taught me the basis of my skill-set today; an amazing experience I am so grateful to have achieved. Post *Harper's Bazaar* I was the Fashion Editor at *Teen Vogue* which was a dream come true. The New York pace was a fast one, something I could do in my twenties without the commitments of children that I have now. I don't think I could manage it all in a similar fashion that I can in Australia. I returned to Sydney when my son Jackson was just six weeks old. I was definitely longing for family and friends along with the lifestyle that Australia brings.

HOME IS WHERE THE HEART IS

Once settling in Australia, I went back to work as the

'Happiness is a happy work–life balance, and happy babies!'

Fashion Editor of *Harper's Bazaar* in Sydney. A more grounding experience than my previous global adventures until Billie came along. Unfortunately I was very ill with her and had to give up work for the time being.

In Australia with two children and a busy life, home is where the heart is. My little family enjoys nights in and my interest in interiors and architecture has grown. When Billie was old enough I went back and studied Interior Design which has lead to my current position as Fashion & Interiors Editor of *Real Living Magazine*.

THE JUGGLE

I learned the hard way with my first born, Jackson, when I tried to achieve too much and essentially burnt out. With Billie I knew from experience that it was all just a phase. I put more of a focus on raising the children in their beautiful infancy than advancing my career and trying to over achieve.

SPECIAL BABY MOMENTS

Meeting my kids for the first time was a huge rush of love and excitement for what our future would be together.

Juggling my career with my kids was a huge learning curve. The sleep deprivation combined with trying to achieve what you previously could in a day before children was a huge adjustment. With my first child Jackson, we learned together. I slowly adjusted to achieving less and putting his needs first. I went back to work when Jackson was three months old. I learned when Billie was born this just was not possible. The baby and I needed time together, time to recover and time to bond as a new family.

Special baby moments include their first words, first friends and becoming more independent. I thought I would never see the day they could dress and feed themselves breakfast. This day has happened . . . exciting times! Nowadays I try to work efficiently in the time they are at school then finish around 5 p.m. so we can do activities, dinner and homework together on an ideal schedule when it works out that way.

MUM ADVICE

The best advice I can give to other mums is to be able to let go of the small things – a tidy house or a pile of washing doesn't really matter. What matters is spending that time focused on your children's needs. Let go of whatever you need to sleep, rest and restore to enable you to do it all again the next day.

HAPPINESS IS . . .

Balance. A happy work–life balance, and happy babies!

Photographer: Donna Griffin

ASHLEA INGRAM

FORMER MISS UNIVERSE AUSTRALIA, YOGA INSTRUCTOR, MUM

'Meeting my children was one of the most special and memorable times of my life. My children are the best gifts I have ever received.'

I had a lovely upbringing, I was very lucky to have wonderful parents who always wanted the best for me and my younger brother. I went to a good school, lived in a beautiful home with a big backyard and a pool, a treehouse my parents built, and a family dog. I remember having a lemonade stall made with lemons from a tree in our backyard, and my mum helping us make a go-cart from scratch. We went on family holidays every school holiday: beach vacations, skiing, trips overseas. I didn't realise how good I had it until I grew up and looked back on how privileged I actually was.

ENTERING THE MODELLING WORLD

I was scouted on the street when I was seventeen by a modelling agency. One of my first big jobs was a parade in fashion week for Bowie Wong. I rode in to the catwalk on the back of a motorbike wearing leather pants and holding a cigarette. I remember suddenly feeling very cool, for someone who was such a dorky teenager!

The man who ran the modelling agency I worked for suggested I enter the Miss Universe Pageant. It was such an incredible experience going into the Miss Universe Pageant. I was at university at the time, and had to be away in Panama for a month for the pageant so my grades sure took a hit that semester, but it was very worth it. That time was my fifteen minutes of fame when I was all of a sudden treated like an absolute rock star. Followed by paparazzi, being in a parade waving to thousands of people, dinner at the President's mansion – it was a lot of fun, and something that not many people get to experience. There wasn't so much a sense of competition between the girls, as one of camaraderie. I made friends from all over the world, and we were all living together so it was like a big, long, extended sleepover with crazy girls. I had a blast. I also got to meet Donald Trump. I had heard some rumours about his behaviour, but I was pleasantly surprised to find him acting totally cordially and respectfully towards me.

'There came a point where I wanted to change my career and focus more on health and wellbeing.'

The best part of being Miss Universe was that it opened doors, and allowed me to meet so many interesting, colourful people. One day I was invited out on the harbour on a friend of a friend's boat, and unbeknownst to me, the cast of a movie filming in Sydney was on it. The next thing I knew I was invited to a dinner party to watch the Oscars with a room full of Hollywood celebrities and I was like, 'Wait – How did I get here?'

INVESTMENT BANKING

After I finally finished university, I thought it was time to put my degree to good use and I went to work as an investment banking analyst. That was a very intense time – our standard work day was from 9 a.m. to around midnight or 1 a.m., sometimes until 4 a.m. It was a very fast-paced, high pressure environment. I was also trying to keep some semblance of a social life too, so I would bring a cocktail dress to work with me, go out for an hour or two and then head back into the office for the remainder of the night. Working for Citigroup and Morgan Stanley was mostly hard work, but the highlight of that time was probably my training in New York City, being around some of the brightest minds and most competitive people in the finance industry. It was quite a change from the modelling world!

EXPANDING THE FAMILY

There came a point when I wanted a change in my career and to focus more on health and wellbeing. Yoga had become something I was really passionate about, and I saw it as a way for me to help others by teaching it.

While I was building up my yoga business, I fell pregnant. I was teaching quite an athletic-style practice, and so the pregnancy obviously threw a bit of a spanner in the works there! I signed up for a pre and postnatal yoga course so I could modify my teaching. I was also modelling, and again – a pregnancy isn't very amenable to that kind of career! I did book a few maternity jobs and showed off my bump.

Photographer: Donna Griffin

MEETING MY CHILDREN

It was one of the most special and memorable times of my life. My children are the best gifts I've ever received. However, meeting them was different for each child. My daughter Camilla was delivered via emergency C-section at 36 weeks, and whisked off to the newborn intensive care unit to be watched over by nurses for the next three weeks. While she melted my heart immediately, the love was mixed with concern. She was so tiny, she was off the bottom of the charts for weight. She has certainly caught up now though – she is a four year old wearing size six clothes, taller than most of the boys in her class! With Lincoln, everything was so much smoother and worry-free. It was instant love and constant cuddles. I was smitten from the very first time I held him.

BACK TO WORK

I found it difficult to find someone to watch Camilla while I went off to teach or do a modelling gig. I leaned on friends a bit, but fortunately in those lines of work, it meant I never had to be away from Camilla for too long. I had a couple of awkward times when I had to take her to castings with me, and once on a shoot with me! The assistants, stylists and hairdressers just kind of took turns passing her around! There was one occasion when a friend was due to watch Camilla while I taught a class, and she went into labour that morning! So again, I had to take the baby with me to the class! It was a corporate class for a naturopathic and vitamin company, and all the girls in the office just took turns looking after Camilla. It was hilarious, but I don't recommend bringing your child to work as a parenting/career balancing strategy!

THE JUGGLE

I handle the juggle these days by relying on kindy and crèches, and family for support. It certainly helps that my husband, Geoff, is very helpful with the children and they just adore spending time with him.

I'm very lucky that yoga is something I love to do, and the schedule is perfect for this time in my life. I can go to work and then come home to my children feeling better than I did before. These days, family has definitely taken priority over career for me. The quote, 'You can have it all, just not all at once,' really resonates with me. My children aren't going to be little forever, and these formative years are the time when they need their mother most. I can return my focus to work once they start school, but just for these few years – my babies come first.

'Make your own kind of music. Sing your own special song.'

ADVICE FROM MY MOTHER

My mother summarises her views on motherhood in the lyrics from a Mamas and the Papas song which encourages you to make your own kind of music and sing your own special song. You have to do what works for you and your family.

MUM ADVICE

The book *The Happiest Baby on the Block* is the best mum advice I've received for soothing and settling newborns. My advice to other mums is to buy a good big handbag! Always carry baby wipes, spare nappy, snacks and water. Try to keep a sense of humour about yourself if you're feeling bogged down by all the mum duties. And most importantly, just make sure your kids feel loved.

HAPPINESS IS ...

There are three places that I am guaranteed to find happiness – running on the beach, on the yoga mat, or inside a warm cuddle with my husband and/or children. Fortunately for me, we live on the beach, I teach yoga, and there is no shortage of cuddles in our house!

THINGS THAT MAKE ME SMILE . . .

The cheeky look on my son's face when he is doing something naughty and looking me right in the eye as he does it. I can't stay mad at him!

Dior

MEGAN HESS

INTERNATIONAL FASHION ARTIST, MUM OF TWO

'What my mother taught me I try to instill in my kids as well, to feel good about themselves and have enormous respect for yourself in order to have respect for others.'

I spent my childhood being very happy, on an acre with lots of animals; it was definitely a very fun childhood! I remember more than anything loving to draw. I don't ever remember not drawing; it was my favourite thing to do. I would go to art classes on the weekends and I felt so free to create, it was like my own private world. I remember being completely happy when I was immersed in drawing and it brought me a lot of joy and calm. Being able to create something was so exciting to me. When it came to choosing a career path, I always knew I wanted to draw but as a child I didn't know that becoming a fashion illustrator was actually a career. I became really interested in the Russian artist Erté. He was one of the first illustrators to illustrate the cover of *Harper's Bazaar* and *Vogue*.

CAREER BREAKTHROUGH

It was like a perfect storm. I had been trying to have a baby and I'd been trying to be a fashion illustrator. I was on the verge of giving up when one night at midnight, I received a call from Candace Bushnell's publisher in New York asking me to illustrate her book cover of *Sex and the City*. It was around this time that I found out I was pregnant as well. My career was completely taking off! I realised when good things come along you just say yes and you take it and you work it all out later.

The biggest challenge at that time was to make it all work. I was so excited that my career had finally taken off but I was also so excited to be a mum – to some extent it will always be a challenge to juggle both, but I think with time you become better at both. I think having children makes you much more decisive when it comes to work because you have children, you don't take on anything unless you really want to. In both areas you really hone your skills and you appreciate every second with your children, especially when you spend a lot of time away

'Nothing is more enjoyable to me than a Sunday barbeque on the deck, my husband and I having a glass of wine while the kids jump around.'

working. I think when I started to look at the juggle as a positive – being a mum and having a great career – I worried less and I started enjoying everything a bit more.

Now it's almost at that point where it's hard to remember what it was like not having children. Children are like one big adventure. Seeing them grow up is like nothing else and they really do give you that sense of achievement. The thing you don't realise before you have children is that you actually get an enormous amount back from them. When they get a bit older, they start to ask how you are; when they see you bewildered and they come over and give you a hug, it's the best feeling in the world. That's what has really changed – having little people you love gives you a heightened sense of purpose. It makes you want to be a good person and a good role model for them.

BACK TO WORK

For me, I didn't really take any maternity leave. It sounds kind of weird but because I worked for myself as an illustrator and didn't have a corporate office, I just kept working through. I had finally built up my business and it was pretty tough, but I felt I didn't really have a choice. I spent ten years building up my work to a point where things had happened. But on the other side, I had complete flexibility. I was drawing things for Dior with my hair in a scrunchie and no make-up and that was the brilliant thing! I could do what I do in between feeds too. It made me realise women can do anything but we need to do it in our own way and that may not work for the rest of the world. But if we are given freedom and flexibility, I really do believe women can do anything.

BABY WEIGHT

It took me about a year per child to lose the weight, but you're so tired and you really don't care. Although after ten months, I decided I wanted to get back in my old clothes. But I really didn't have time with a newborn to enter into a really big exercise routine. So I would just walk up and down the steps everyday. I had 100 stairs in my apartment building and I would do a couple of rounds every day. Just doing regular exercise and eating well helped me to eventually get back to my pre-pregnancy weight.

THE JUGGLE

My daughter is now twelve and my son is eight, so I feel more secure in how I do things. They are really happy, kind, lovely kids. Obviously they have their moments but I probably shouldn't have worried so much at the beginning and I should have just trusted my gut. But as a new mum you are fraught with different opinions. For me, taking on a lot of things that I did, and taking it all on at once, actually worked for me and my family. The juggle is something I've come to expect will always be there. When none of us are sick and I've got my deadlines done, the kids have their homework done and we are all able to have a laugh at some point during the day then it is a complete success.

THE CHALLENGES

I've had loads of challenges. Before I began working on incredible brands like Fendi, Prada and Dior, I worked for years on projects that I certainly wasn't passionate about, for example a horse manual, which they actually shut down and never used after six months of work! I could name lots of soul-destroying projects, but I now I look back and realise that every single project I worked on, I got something back from and they make me appreciate all the things now. All the challenges I have faced have brought me to a place where I now appreciate the little things. Another challenge I faced was trying to publish a children's book. It took me ten years! Over the years I had lots of meetings with publishers and they just weren't sure about my ideas. Now I look back and see that those ideas I had in the past probably did suck and probably weren't that good. By failing at those ideas but keeping the spirit alive in hoping it will happen someday, that's what has lead to me so what has finally gone right, with my first children's book, *Claris: The Chicest Mouse in Paris*.

CAREER HIGHLIGHT

The recent project I did for Fendi has been a career highlight because to work on a project curated by Karl Lagerfeld is such a dream come true. It basically began with me flying to Milan and sketching live at their show. From there, Fendi asked me to sketch a series of images for a global campaign. From there they asked me to sketch an animation. They gave me freedom to do whatever I thought creatively, and when I pitched them a 'Fendi Fairytale,' I couldn't believe it that out of all the illustrators in the world, they chose me to do the campaign.

FAMILY TIME

I love the basics! Nothing is more enjoyable to me than a Sunday barbeque on the deck, my husband and I having a glass of wine while the kids are jumping around and we're all just hanging out. Other than that, I love when we get to travel together. Our favourite place is Hawaii so each year we try to get there and it's just the most relaxing holiday. So just being together is the best.

But during the week it's like Heathrow airport at our house. I'm Skyping early in the morning with people all over the world. My studio is metres from my house, so I walk down to my studio, I get straight into the working day and I love it. It's one of those feelings that I have where I get to appreciate what I do for a job. I have that flutter of excitement every day. I have about ten projects at once. I work with a team of incredibly talented women. And that's the other thing – being able to work with other women and have that shared experience is a lot more fun than working on my own. Plus every day is completely different. By the afternoon the kids are home from school, we're doing homework and there's dinner. My husband and I enjoy a glass of wine, although sometimes we're so tired we can barely share our day! But I think that's a nice time to share something with my husband. And I think it's important to remember the relationship with your partner is just as important. Then I end every day with a hot bath – whether it's summer or winter, it's my ritual and then I'm usually ready to pass out.

HEALTH AND WELLBEING

I wish I could say I was a healthy person – I want to be but like a lot of working mums you do what you can. I am not a brilliant cook but I try and do what I can. But I continue to meditate. I started about six years ago and found it to be the most effective thing I can do to feel calm and balanced. I think every mum gets overwhelmed at times with so many things to be doing at once, even the stuff you're really excited about, but I've found just putting aside twenty minutes a day really makes a huge difference. It's like rebooting your computer. I do try and eat as healthily as I can . . . but I have a huge sweet tooth!

ROLE MODELS

My grandmother and my mum are definitely my role models because growing up they were very strong women who always made me feel like whatever I wanted to do in life I could do. There was never any pressure for me to get married, have kids or have a traditional career. They gave me a lot of confidence and always believed in me – I have the courage to do that.

SUCCESS IS . . .

Genuinely being happy. Happiness for me is also waking up on a Monday morning and being able to come and draw in the studio because I have created a life where I am somehow paid for what I would do in my spare time anyway. Being a mum and having happy, healthy, kids is also the biggest and most successful thing to me in life.

MY MOTHER TAUGHT ME . . .

Every good thing in my life my mother taught me. I find myself saying things to my daughter thinking that is what my mum would have said. Above all, she taught me not to give up in what I believe in. But as a little shy kid who didn't feel confident or that the world was my oyster, she told me I could do anything if I put my mind to it, and that anything is possible. She always reassured me that I could do anything and I try and instill this in my kids as well – to feel good about themselves and have enormous respect for yourself in order to have respect for others.

Photographer: Chantel Bianchi

SAMANTHA BRETT

BESTSELLING AUTHOR, TV REPORTER, MUM

'No matter who the mum, what she does or where she's from, we're all in the same boat. We are all juggling. We are all struggling with the juggling, but we are all making it work as best we can.'

I grew up in Johannesburg, South Africa during a time when it was often too dangerous to go to the local park, so family, siblings and our backyard became my entire world. I was never the maternal type. My husband was very keen for a big family but I was enjoying focusing on my career as a news reporter, journalist and author to make time for much else. But as the years went by, priorities shifted!

I was heavily pregnant when my seventh book came out, *The Game Changers*, featuring an exclusive interview with Meghan Markle. We had worked so long on the book that it was like giving birth when it was finally printed. The subject matter also meant that the world wanted a piece of myself and my co-author Steph Adams. So despite being tired, swollen and very, very hungry, I went out and did media interviews, book signings and shipped off books (often carrying multiple heavy boxes to and from the post office much to the shock of onlookers) to send to people eager to get their hands on a copy.

When Harper was born, I had also been working as a court reporter for Channel Seven covering courts and crime; often the worst in humanity. It was a shock at first to take a break from the hustle and bustle. I had never taken off much time from work since I started in the media industry when I was eighteen years old and had just kept going, going, going, working all over the world, dedicating everything I had to my work and advancing my career. Working early mornings, late nights, every weekend for as long as I can remember.

Harper came into the world fashionably early. She was the most beautiful baby I had ever seen, although I had never actually seen or held a newborn before!

Of the early days I remember the focus was just on keeping Harper alive. I read every book, blog and article that I could get my hands on with the hopes of finding out every bit of information about motherhood that I possibly could, and then quickly realising that no matter how much material you read, it's really all about

Photographer: Chantel Bianchi

'Harper came into the world fashionably early. She was the most beautiful baby I had ever seen.'

'I'm grateful for the shift in focus because I think you grow as a person, a mum, a colleague and definitely as a journalist when you're so heavily contributing to the life of someone else.'

trial and error in the end, and making your own mistakes.

I found the first three months the most difficult mentally, emotionally and physically as well as extremely messy! With pooh explosions, spit ups, sleepless nights and constant worry, but once the first three months were over, I could finally relax a little bit and start to really enjoy my time with Harper.

I went back to work after four months, trying to juggle it all with office time scheduled in for early mornings and late nights so I could have as much time with Harper as possible. Thankfully my job as a news reporter isn't about being in the office from nine to five (more like starting work at 3:30 a.m.) and my husband was able to pick up a lot of the slack so I could get back to work. And thankfully I don't need much sleep!

The Juggle is real. Your life is no longer just about you. I can't just pick up and head off to the latest breaking news around the world and not know when I'll be home. Time is now of the essence and every minute has to be used wisely. When I'm with Harper, I try and give her my undivided attention and leave work to one side for a moment, even if there is a work issue that urgently needs my attention.

I'm grateful for the shift in focus because I think you grow as a person, a mum, a colleague and definitely as a journalist when you're so heavily contributing to the life of someone else rather than constantly thinking of me, me, me. Yes, my hair is nowadays no longer perfectly coiffed and clean, nail polish is always chipped, there's barely any time for a shower, gym has gone completely out the window and I can't remember the last time I had a leg wax.

But it's these early days for me that I know will be the most precious when I look back on it all. I've certainly managed to work full time, write a new book and be a very present mum too, but not without some serious help from family and friends, and lots of very, very strong coffee!

What has surprised me the most about The Juggle is that no matter who the mum, how successful they are or how many kids they have, we're all in the same boat; we're all juggling. We're all struggling with the juggling, but we're all making it work as best we can.

I have a newfound respect and admiration for all mums, but especially single mothers and mothers doing it tough. They are the true heroes and reading their stories while putting this book together has given me so much joy, and we hope – so much inspiration to other women.

Photographer: Chantel Bianchi

Photographer: Mark Stanley

Photographer: Chantel Bi

STEPH ADAMS

BESTSELLING AUTHOR, ART DIRECTOR, EDITOR, MUM

'It's such a surreal moment when you meet this little person for the first time. I just remember this incredible love and this noisy little baby I just wanted to protect.'

My childhood growing up in Perth was wonderful and I remember mornings and afternoons spent at Cottesloe Beach. My mother and I would often walk around Peppermint Grove foreshore, there was always the lovely smell of peppermint trees.

Our families would often meet at my grandfather's house on the Esplanade, overlooking the Swan River every Christmas where my cousins and I would tear up the lawn playing chasy. We were always running and playing at the river or the beach, spending time camping up to Broome, playing in the pool with my sister, family vacations down south and summer barbecues spent outside laughing as a family together. It was fairly magical.

My grandfather, Phillip Adams. Q.C was always someone I looked up to as a child. He had a lot of presence. Most people would stop to look up if he ever walked into a room. I wanted to be just like him.

During the time he was bringing the drinking age down from 21 to 18 in Australia, my father would be out having under-age parties and my grandfather would be the one having to go to the police station to fetch him. It's something our family can all laugh about now, but I'm sure it caused him a lot of distress at the time. All the joys of parenting!

Drawing and painting was what I enjoyed most at school but when the time came to choose a career, I worried that I would not make any money as an artist, which is why I switched to graphic design and continued a career towards art direction in the publishing industry.

My first job as a graphic designer was at *Vogue* Australia in Sydney after a decade of modelling with Vivien's Models and around the world. After the experience at *Vogue*, I received a call to come in and work at *Marie Claire* as a freelance designer. After a few weeks they offered me the position of art director. That experience paved the way toward working in London with *British Vogue*, *Net-a-Porter, Harper's Bazaar UK*, *Elle UK* and *Condé Nast Traveler*. All this experience together brought me to ultimately publish books. My first book was *Good to Glow* which I co-authored, a healthy recipe book. It was the perfect time as I had just became pregnant with my first son Bailey.

I started a design studio, Steph Adams Creative, in 2008 alongside working full time. I was designing branding for skin care and packaging for various celebrities, as well as producing wine labels, brochures, logos, business cards and coffee-table books.

In 2009, I started blogging on the side of running a design business. I was interviewing different women as

'Parenting teaches you patience and children have a way of putting you in your place.'

'I met my husband nine years ago. I knew he was the one on our second date in South Africa. There was just this sense of calm about him. He has been my biggest supporter and rock ever since.'

well as my clients about their brands. The blog started to attract a lot of attention and slowly built a very large following. It opened up a lot of doors and enabled me to meet various women around the world who had become successful in their own right. This paved the way for my books; *Good to Glow*, *The Game Changers* and *The Juggle*.

My husband and I met nine years ago. I knew he was The One on our second date in South Africa. There was just a sense of calm about him. We were engaged after only four months. He has been my biggest supporter and rock ever since. It's been a wonderful love story. It's only now that I look back, I see that every little path you take brings you to where you are supposed to be. You always have to follow your intuition and never listen to what others say.

It was a special and exciting time when we fell pregnant with Bailey, as it was our first, and I was working on my first health book as a first-time author.

I enjoyed most of the pregnancy until the last month and then I was just so ready for the baby to come out. Pregnancy forces you to look after yourself in every way.

When Bailey first came along, he was a month early and no one was quite prepared, including my husband. When they told him he was coming that night, he almost fainted. It is such a surreal moment when you meet this little person for the first time. I just remember this incredible love and this little noisy baby that I just wanted to love and protect.

Joshua also came a month early and it was right when my co-author, Samantha Brett, and I were working on the second edition of *The Game Changers*. Nothing prepares you more for number two – one child is like one and two is like having ten kids!

Our book was making headlines all around the world because of the Meghan Markle interview and I was in this baby la la land and toddler bubble!

When the book launch came, Josh was only six weeks and Bailey was three-years-old and I remember arriving so unbelievably tired to a media wall of cameras and film crews, and then giving a speech along with the Hon. Julia Bishop MP. We also had a line-up of TV interviews and radio interviews. It was a crazy time! But

Photography: Sugarlight Photography

you can never plan these things, you just have to sort of ride the wave and wing it, so to speak.

One of the craziest times Samantha and I had during the promotion for *The Game Changers* was almost missing a TV interview with a UK news network for the Royal Wedding of Prince Harry and Meghan Markle. We literally arrived one hour late and they still let us in! I guess in among all the chaos there will always be moments of laughter.

Since having two children and starting *Laqua magazine*, my life has changed in many ways. I've had to cancel overseas work trips that I would have loved to have attended because my children needed me. You definitely don't have as much freedom just to take off like you did before. Without kids, however, you wouldn't have the small joys in life either – the moments that warm your heart.

My favourite moment as a family was only recently when we were in Barcelona running through the airport about to miss our plane. My husband was running way ahead of us and Bailey only a few metres in front of me. I was carrying Josh who was laughing hysterically at Bailey trying to run with his nappy coming off, until it finally did. It was one of those moments when you just love being a family.

Photographer: Sugarlight Photography

Photographer: Sugarlight Photography

Photographer: Sugarlight Photography

GM Photographics

NOT ALL WHO WANDER ARE LOST; SOME ARE JUST MUMS HIDING FROM THEIR CHILDREN.

THE JUGGLE

THE ART OF THE
JUGGLE

Our experts give you their top tips on how to navigate motherhood

Photography by Chantel Bianchi

THE JUGGLE EXPERTS

As evidenced from the stories throughout this book, no matter who the woman is, how successful she may be, where she is from or her parenting style, The Juggle is real. The Juggle struggle is faced by mums around the world, as we all try to navigate the most important job of our lives: bringing up our children as best we can.

But, there are times during The Juggle when women simply need help. It's tough. It's draining. We get run down, exhausted, sick and sometimes mental health issues enter into the equation too.

While putting together this book, we've spent the past year canvassing and questioning the experts in their fields to bring you some empowering tools to help you with your Juggle.

Whether it's knowing the tricks and tools to getting veggies and probiotics into your child, looking after your own health with easy-to-cook recipes, taking care of your body with exercises you can do while holding your bub in your hands, or of course, looking after your state of mind, we hope these tips and tricks will help make your Juggle a little more manageable.

THE IMPORTANCE OF NUTRITION FOR KIDS

MANDY SACHER

CHILD NUTRITION EXPERT, AUTHOR

When I had my son, I realised how much help and guidance new parents need around family nutrition. I became increasingly aware of the lack of appropriate information out there, and what was available was often very conflicting and confusing. Wholesome Child was founded to provide simple and effective strategies to guide parents on how to give their children the best nutritional start in life. As my consulting practice grew, my focus shifted from my one-on-one Wholesome Child clinic consultations to include group workshops and then I published *Wholesome Child: A Complete Nutrition Guide and Cookbook*, in an effort to reach and help more families. I really believe in taking a preventative approach to children's health. Let's face it, parenthood isn't easy, but if we can get the basics like food and sleep in place, it makes life so much easier.

NUTRITION FOR KIDS

I know firsthand that getting the foundations right for healthy eating is so important. I firmly believe that healthy nutrition for children is the best way to ensure their long-term health. A wholefood diet rich in quality proteins, healthy fats, wholegrains and a diverse range of vegetables is likely to benefit your child in numerous ways – including a reduced risk of obesity, hypertension and tooth cavities, plus improvements in their immunity and gut health – and may also benefit them psychologically too. Educating little tastebuds early on to appreciate wholefoods in their natural state, free from additives, flavourings and preservatives nurtures a positive attitude and, hopefully, trains children to enjoy a healthy diet throughout their lives. So often the behaviours and the relationship towards food is cemented in childhood. Of the families that come to my clinic, I see how hard it is for children to increase their limited diets when their parents are fussy eaters too. There are so many psychological disadvantages of not having a healthy diet. Before I worked with children, I was in adult health where I saw that once those negative associations and behaviours like yo-yo dieting, self-loathing and a poor relationship towards food are already established, it's very hard to turn it around. That's why I'm so passionate about getting the foundations right from the start.

'Main meals should contain a serve of quality protein, one to two serves of a slow-release carbohydrate, two to three vegetables.'

HOW CAN BUSY MUMS MAKE SURE KIDS EAT HEALTHY?

Very often parents receive the message that it's an all-or-nothing approach – that you have to cook everything from scratch, you have to be the perfect parent to get things right and that's simply not the case. One thing that I'm always keen to stress to families is the importance of learning how to read and decipher nutrition labels, so that when you do rely on store-bought products, you're actually purchasing the right ones. Clever marketing means that it's easy to miss nasties like MSG and sugars hiding behind a different name and a product that appears healthy can often be anything but. Interpreting nutrition labels and identifying hidden nasties is something I go into in great depth in my book. Something I'm also really passionate about is helping brands and trying to disrupt the children's food market to ensure that there are healthy products on offer for time-poor parents, because right now there simply isn't enough choice in the market.

Often I see mothers who are constantly on diets and have poor self-images, and they're trying to raise healthy kids. It really starts with role modelling and being a healthy example. Little ones are sponges and are incredibly impressionable. Seeing other family members enjoying healthy wholefoods, celebrating their health, their bodies and discussing how important wellbeing is, are all crucial. In addition to this, being involved in food preparation processes and knowing to expect nutritious foods at snack and mealtimes will guide them on a lifelong path of health and wellbeing. It's definitely more of a marathon than a race! And remember, don't expect to get everything right, and go easy on yourself. If you're going to sneak food behind your child's back, just be real about it. There's time to eat cake and there's time to have healthy food. Normalise it. And bring in the fun and enjoyment – include little ones in menu planning and involve them in the shopping and preparation. Let your children know that you enjoy food and they will follow.

DO'S AND DON'TS OF NUTRITION FOR KIDS

Main meals should contain a serve of quality protein, one to two serves of a slow-release carbohydrate, two to three vegetables (aim for a variation of colours for maximum phytonutrient benefit) and a single serve of a healthy fat. I generally recommend that fruit be included as a morning or afternoon snack, rather than included with main meals such as the school lunchbox. I also advise parents that fruit shouldn't be used as a substitute for veggies. Vegetables are nature's insurance policy against disease and so it's worth persisting with encouraging vegetable intake (as challenging as it may be!). Setting children up with a genuine appreciation of wholefoods and vegetables is so important.

Sugar and salt are both addictive and disrupt normal taste sensations, and leading to cravings which can have long-term health implications, so try to always keep healthy and nutritious food options in plain view and remove junk food as much as possible. What the eyes see, the tummy wants, and this is as true for adults as it is for children. Involving children in the grocery shopping, meal preparation and eating together as a family, no matter how infrequently, are all going to help establish healthy habits.

SUPPLEMENTS FOR KIDS

While it is the ideal for kids to get their daily nutritional requirements from food, if required, probiotics, high quality fish oil, vitamin D, zinc, magnesium and vitamin C at appropriate and recommended doses may be suitable for children. And obviously iron if they need it. But the best way to boost children's immunity is with natural, non-processed foods high in vitamins and minerals, and probiotic-rich foods. Goji and cherries may help to promote a healthy immune system.

Oily fish like wild salmon, sardines and mackerel contain omega-3 oils, an important anti-inflammatory for the whole body. They also contain selenium and vitamin E – important immune system strengtheners.

Dark green leafy vegetables like Brussels sprouts, spinach and kale are packed with essential vitamins and minerals which can help boost the body's natural healing powers. The real super vegetable is broccoli which contains an abundant supply of antioxidants, vitamin C, calcium, iron, beta-carotene and folate.

We now know that gut health is important for

'The best way to boost children's immunity is with natural, non-processed foods high in vitamins and minerals.'

a healthy immune system and probiotic-rich foods are essential to improving and maintain good gut bacteria. Keffir yoghurt is packed with probiotics and now readily available at specialty and health food stores. The taste is a bit tart so best to add it to your child's normal yoghurt in small doses to start off with, or add it to smoothies. Other probiotic rich foods include kombucha, bone broth, kim chi and natural yoghurt.

Keep junk food and unhealthy sweets to a minimum. They may well impact on your child's microbiome and in turn your child's digestion and wider health.

Also, remember that letting kids grub around in the mud and play with animals is a great way to strengthen their immune systems, and that antibacterial wipes and disinfectants may be responsible for altering the gut microbiome in a manner harmful to human health.

ENCOURAGING HEALTHY EATING PATTERNS

Teaching your children to cook sets them up with fantastic skills that will last them a lifetime. Not to mention the fact that they are much more likely to try meals they have helped to prepare themselves. Countless studies show that eating meals regularly as a family provides numerous, lasting benefits that go far beyond simple nutrition. Adolescents who eat with their family four or more times a week do better at school, are less likely to engage in underage drinking and have less social and emotional problems. This can be difficult for some families to achieve every day, so aim to start off slowly with two to three family meals a week (working on achieving more wherever possible). During family meals, focus on connecting and enjoying family time together – put a ban on devices and TV at the table.

The other important thing to be aware of is how you speak to your child about food, and being conscious of your own attitudes towards it. Are you guilty of comfort eating? Do you have a negative body image? Believe me, your kids have already picked up on these things so it's crucial that as parents we speak positively about food around children.

Instead of talking about food in terms of high and low calories, try to discuss it in terms of its healthy attributes – so for instance, fish oil is good for your brain, carrot can be good for eyesight, and too many lollies or doughnuts might upset your tummy. For older kids you can explain this in more detail. Also, talk about your body in terms of strength and never speak negatively about your own weight or about body dissatisfaction in front of children. Also, teach kids to identify when they are hungry, thirsty or full and try not to let them eat out of boredom or for emotional reasons. Constantly praise your child for making healthy choices and avoid making your child feel guilty about their food choices.

'Teaching your children to cook sets them up with fantastic skills that will last them a lifetime.'

HEALTHY RECIPES YOUR KIDS WILL LOVE

SWEET POTATO PIZZA

Nut-free, Egg-free.
Prep time: 20 mins Cooking time: 30 mins Makes: 1 pizza

Kids love pizza but they don't always go for vegetable toppings. So I decided to create a pizza for my kids which had veggies in the base – and it worked best with sweet potato. Rich in beta carotene and fibre, sweet potatoes are a great addition to a pizza base.

INGREDIENTS
Dough:
1½ cups (375g) sweet potato, peeled, steamed and mashed
1½ cups (210g) wholemeal spelt flour
2 tsp baking powder
1 tsp salt
1 tbs extra virgin olive oil
1 tsp oregano (dried)

Topping:
1 cup (250g) tomato paste or passata
2 cups (160g) grated cheese (cheddar, mozzarella or feta)
optional extras: basil, mushrooms, capsicum, tomatoes, olives, grated carrot, grated zucchini, anchovies

INSTRUCTIONS
1. Preheat oven to 200°C/400°F and line a pizza pan or baking tray with baking paper.
2. To make the dough, place all ingredients into a high-speed food processor and process until well combined. Or you can add the ingredients to a large bowl and knead well together with your hands until the mixture resembles a ball of orange pizza dough.
3. Press out the dough into a large circle. If it's too sticky, oil your hands with olive oil. To achieve a crispy base, the dough should be about a 0.5cm thick.
4. Bake in the oven for approximately 15–20 mins or until the edges of the dough are slightly browned. 20 mins will ensure a crisp base.
5. Remove pizza base from oven, spread over the tomato paste or passata, sprinkle with cheese and preferred toppings, and grill for 5–8 mins until cheese has melted.
6. Allow to cool, then cut into slices.

Serving and storing leftovers: Serve immediately. Store in the fridge for up to 4 days or freeze the precooked base for up to 4 months.
Tip: Great for school lunch boxes. For a gluten-free version, use 1½ cups buckwheat flour, 1 cup almond meal and 1 tsp psyllium husk powder instead of the 2 cups of spelt flour.

Recipe credit from Mandy Sacher, Wholesome Child

WHOLESOME CHILD SUPERCHARGED BOLOGNAISE

Dairy-free, Nut-free, Gluten-free, Egg-free.

Prep time: 20 mins Cooking time: 45 mins Serves: 8

Even the fussiest of eaters won't be able to detect the veggies in this dish. It can be pureed into a smooth consistency for babies and picky eaters.

INGREDIENTS

1–2 tbs coconut oil
1 large brown onion, finely chopped
2–4 cloves garlic, finely crushed
1kg beef or lamb mince
2 tbs mixed Italian herbs (dried)
2 tsp ground cinnamon
700g tomato passata in a glass bottle (not canned)
1 cup (250ml) vegetable stock or bone broth
½ cup (125g) butternut pumpkin, steamed and pureed (reserve steaming water)
½ cup (125g) sweet potato, steamed and pureed
2 dried apricots, sulphur-free, finely sliced
1 cup (25g) spinach, finely chopped
sea salt and black pepper, to taste

INSTRUCTIONS

1. In a large pot, heat oil on medium heat and sauté onion and garlic until transparent.
2. Add mince, then turn up the heat and brown.
3. Sprinkle the mixed herbs and cinnamon over the mince. Keep stirring until mince is browned all the way through and no pink pieces can be seen.
4. Pour in tomato passata and vegetable stock, cover and simmer covered on low heat for 10 mins.
5. Add butternut, sweet potato and apricots, recover and simmer for 15 mins.
6. Stir in spinach and check to make sure liquid level is not too low. If extra water is needed, add water from steamed vegetables to increase vitamin and mineral content. Simmer for 10 more mins.
7. Add salt and pepper to taste.

Serving and storing leftovers: Serve immediately, store in fridge for up to 3 days or freeze for up to 4 months.

Tip: Serve with wholegrain spaghetti, buckwheat noodles, brown rice or quinoa.

Recipe credit from Mandy Sacher, Wholesome Child

600ml
500ml

'This delicious watermelon cake is a great alternative to sugar-filled cakes.'

WATERMELON CAKE

Nut-free, Gluten-free, Egg-free, Vegetarian friendly, Wheat-free.
Prep time: 30 mins Serves: 15–20

This delicious watermelon cake is a great alternative to sugar-filled cakes. When my daughter turned two and started daycare we served a watermelon cake for her birthday. The kids loved it, the teachers thought it was the best idea ever and parents were amazed at how quickly it disappeared!

INGREDIENTS

1 large seedless watermelon (7–9kg)
1–2 cups (250–500ml) whipping cream (depends on the size of your watermelon)
½ tsp vanilla extract or powder (optional)
seasonal fresh fruit (optional)

INSTRUCTIONS

1. Remove the top and bottom from the watermelon as well as the rind from the middle section. You should be left with a cake-shaped piece of watermelon.
2. Pat the outside of the watermelon dry with paper towels. This is a very important step as it helps the whipped cream adhere to the watermelon.
3. In a large bowl, whip the cream until stiff. Gently fold in vanilla extract or paste, if using.
4. Frost the watermelon cake with the whipped cream and top with your favourite fruits and berries, or serve without.

Serving and storing leftovers: Serve immediately or store in the fridge for up to 3 days.

Recipe credit from Mandy Sacher, Wholesome Child

BANANA BREAD

Dairy-free, Nut-free, Vegetarian Friendly, Wheat-free.
Prep time: 15 minutes Cooking time: 55 mins Quantity: Makes 1 loaf

Store-bought banana breads are often overloaded with processed flours, sugars and unhealty fats. This far healhtier version contains wholegrain spelt flour, a reduced amount of unprocessed sugar, coconut oil and chia seeds.

INGREDIENTS
2 large ripe bananas
3 large eggs
½ cup (125ml) coconut milk
4–6 Medjool dates, pitted
1 tbs chia seeds
½ cup (125ml) coconut oil, melted
1½ cups (210g) wholemeal spelt flour
⅓–½ cup (55–75g) coconut sugar
1 tsp vanilla powder or extract
1 tsp ground cinnamon, plus extra
1 tsp baking powder
½ tsp baking soda
pinch of sea salt

INSTRUCTIONS
1. Preheat oven to 180°C/350°F and line a medium-sized loaf tin with baking paper.
2. Place bananas, eggs, milk, dates, chia seeds and coconut oil in a high-speed blender and process for approximately 1 min or until it reaches a smooth consistency.
3. In a separate bowl whisk together spelt flour, coconut sugar, vanilla powder, cinnamon, baking powder, baking soda and salt.
4. Slowly add dry ingredients to wet mixtrure and mix together on a medium speed. Pour mixture into the loaf tin and sprinkle extra cinnamon on top.
5. Bake for approximately 45–55 mins or until a cake tester or knife comes out clean.
Allow to cool completely before cutting.

Serving and storing leftovers: Serve immediately, store in an airtight container in the fridge for up to a week or freeze for up to 4 months.

Recipe credit from Mandy Sacher, Wholesome Child

RICH CHOCOLATE BLACK BEAN BROWNIES

Vegetarian, Gluten-free, Dairy-free, Nut-free

Prep Time: 10 minutes Cooking Time: 25–30 minutes Makes: 16 Mini Brownies

It's hard to believe that the base of this chocolatey goodness is made from black beans, making them high in folate and a good source of iron and fibre.

INGREDIENTS

1½ cups (270g) cooked black beans or 1 x 400g canned black beans rinsed and drained
3 eggs
3 tbs coconut oil, plus a little more for coating the baking dish
⅓ cup (30g) cacao powder
2 tbs carob powder
pinch of sea salt
3 tsp vanilla powder or extract
1 tsp baking powder
½ cup (75g) coconut sugar (to sweeten further, add an extra ¼ cup (35g) coconut sugar or a pinch of stevia)

INSTRUCTIONS

1. Preheat oven to 160°C/320°F.
2. Grease a square 20cm x 20cm baking dish with coconut oil.
3. Place all the ingredients in a food processor and process at a high speed until smooth.
4. Pour the mixture into the prepared baking dish.
5. Place in oven and bake for 25–30 mins. Check after 25 mins by sliding a knife into the brownie. If it comes away clean, it's ready. Allow to cool before cutting into little squares.

Serving and storing leftovers: Serve immediately, store in fridge for 4 days or freeze for up to 4 months. Serve with coconut cream and fresh strawberries for a dessert treat.

Recipe credit from Mandy Sacher, Wholesome Child

THE HEALTHY LIFE POST PREGNANCY

WITH JESS SEPEL, NUTRITIONIST

FOR MANY MULTI-TASKING MUMS, HEALTHY LIVING IS THE LAST THING ON THEIR MINDS. EXPERT NUTRITIONIST JESS SEPEL HELPS BUSY MUMS LIVE THE HEALTHY LIFE, TO GIVE YOU MORE ENERGY, VITALITY, ZEST AND RADIANCE. THESE ARE HER TOP TIPS TO GET BACK INTO SHAPE AFTER BABY ... WITHOUT PRESSURE AND WITH BALANCE!

I believe that health is a lifestyle, not a passing trend. My food philosophy revolves around nourishing wholefoods, mindful eating and moderate indulgence. Our signature method allows you to achieve long-term weight balance while treating yourself to the foods that will help your body thrive.

GIVE UP THE SCALES AND STOP COUNTING CALORIES!

When it comes to getting into shape, the first thing to know is that there's no need to feel pressured or overwhelmed. When our bodies produce too much cortisol and adrenaline – the stress hormones – they can send us into overdrive and even prevent us reaching a balanced, healthy weight. It might sound counterintuitive, but if you're looking to shift some weight, giving up the scales can be incredibly powerful. Why, you ask? Focusing on our weight can lead to an unhealthy relationship with our bodies. Rather than focusing on your weight, try to focus on your mental, physical and emotional health. Ensure you nurture your relationship with yourself and practise self-love. This means doing everything with kindness, flexibility and balance. Rather than counting calories, try to focus on eating good-quality wholefoods, exercising moderately, reducing stress and striving for equilibrium through diet and lifestyle.

EAT THE JSHEALTH WAY

This means enjoying wholefoods and the important macronutrients: protein, fibre, good fats and complex carbohydrates. It also means avoiding processed and packaged foods, and indulging moderately.

CLEANSE YOUR LIVER

Your liver processes all of your hormones and when it's having to process excess alcohol, caffeine and medication, its efficiency is impacted. Up your intake of seasonal vegetables, fresh fruits, gluten-free grains, nuts, seeds, sustainable fish, organic eggs and chicken. Reduce your intake of alcohol, dairy, refined sugar, sweeteners, wheat, gluten and red meat.

BALANCE OUT YOUR NERVOUS SYSTEM

Don't overdo it with exercise or anything too intense. Listen to your body and strike a balance between the yin and yang, which is gentle energy and high energy.

REGULATE YOUR INSULIN AND GLUCOSE LEVELS

Good food choices will help you feel fuller for longer and avoid overeating, so keep your blood sugar in check by choosing dishes that contain protein and good fats, and avoid refined carbohydrates and refined sugar.

NORMALISE YOUR LEPTIN LEVELS

Leptin is an appetite control hormone that sends a signal to your brain when you're full. If you have too much insulin in the body, it can block the leptin hormone, which can lead to overeating. People with high-sugar diets tend to overeat because they can't control when they should stop. To bring your leptin levels into balance, work on eating more protein at each meal. Also, stop eating when you're 80 per cent full and wait 20 minutes before reaching for more food.

BREATHE DEEPLY

Commit to a breathing practice as part of your morning routine. Deep breathing activates the parasympathetic nervous system, which aids happiness, decreases stress, supports immune function, decreases pain and lowers anxiety and cortisol.

BALANCE YOUR THYROID

Ask your doctor to check your thyroid function and include dietary and lifestyle practices to support thyroid support.

PRACTICE YOGA

It's a very calming, restorative practice that works wonders for mind, body and soul.

Photography by Chantel Bianchi

JESSICA SEPEL

NUTRITIONIST, AUTHOR

'After years of suffering with fad dieting, calorie counting and body image issues, I discovered my love for nutrition and transformed my lifestyle. Instead of feeling hateful of my body, I'm now grateful for it. Instead of counting calories, I focus on nourishing wholefoods. I'm passionate about empowering people to give up dieting, throw out the scales and find balance with food for life. I've launched JSHealth App to provide people with access to the simple, realistic and sustainable lifestyle that has helped more than a million people revolutionise their health.'

JESS SEPEL'S RECIPES

JESS SEPEL'S OAT & CINNAMON BREAKFAST COOKIES

Dairy-free, Wheat-free, Egg-free, Vegetarian, Vegan.
Prep time: 10 mins Cooking time: 20 mins Makes: 8–10

I love cookies, especially when they are nutritionally balanced, delicious and hot out of the oven. These crunchy morsels are full of slow-releasing carbohydrates, healthy fats and fibre. They're a great on-the-go breakfast or snack.

INGREDIENTS
1 cup rolled wheat-free oats
2 tbsp chia seeds
⅓ cup desiccated coconut
¼ cup sunflower or pumpkin seeds
⅓ cup raw almonds
½ tsp cinnamon
2 heaped tbsp hulled tahini
2 tbsp stevia powder or maple syrup or raw honey
a big pinch of sea salt
2 dates, pitted (optional)
¼ cup warm water

To serve:
pinch of cinnamon
tahini, to taste

METHOD
1. Preheat oven to 180°C/360°F. Line a baking tray with baking paper.
2. Mix all ingredients in a food processor until it forms a sticky mixture. If it's too dry, add a touch more water.
3. Spoon 1 tbsp of mixture on to the baking tray and shape into a circle. Repeat with remaining mixture.
4. Bake for 15–17 mins until golden around the edges.
5. Drizzle with extra tahini and a sprinkle of cinnamon, if desired.

Serving and storing leftovers: Serve immediately, or store in an airtight container for up to 3 days.

JESS SEPEL'S 3-STEP BANANA & CINNAMON PANCAKES

Dairy-free, Vegetarian.

Prep time: 10 mins   Cooking time: 20 mins   Serves: 2

These pancakes are super fast, delicious and nutritious. Simply blitz the ingredients, fry the pancakes and serve.

INGREDIENTS

Pancakes:

½ cup rolled oats
1 egg
1 tbsp chia seeds
1 banana
1 tsp baking powder
1 tsp cinnamon
¼ cup almond milk
1 tsp coconut oil

Topping:

handful of raw nuts
½ banana, sliced
1 tsp maple syrup (optional)

METHOD

1. To make the pancakes, place all of the ingredients, except the coconut oil, into a blender or food processor. Blitz until you've reached a smooth consistency.
2. Heat the coconut oil in non-stick frying pan over medium heat. Add 2 tbsp of pancake mixture to the pan and fry for 2–3 mins on each side, or until the pancakes are golden and cooked through. Repeat with the rest of the batter
3. To serve, stack the pancakes on a plate and top with freshly sliced banana, raw nuts and maple syrup, if desired.

Serving and storing leftovers: Serve immediately, or wrap cooled pancakes in foil and freeze for up to 1 month.

JESS SEPEL'S SWEET POTATO COTTAGE PIE

Egg-free, Wheat-free, Nut-free, Gluten-free.

Prep time: 20 mins Cooking time: 40 mins Serves: 6

A JSHealth version of an old classic. Warming, hearty and family friendly. This is a great meal to cook up on a Sunday as there is sure to be leftovers!

INGREDIENTS

1 tbsp olive oil
1 brown onion, peeled and finely diced
2 celery stalks, diced
2 carrots, peeled and diced
2 garlic cloves, peeled and finely diced
500g grass-fed organic beef mince
1 x 400g tin brown lentils, rinsed and drained
1 x 400g tin diced tomatoes, no added salt
1 tbsp good quality tomato paste, no sugar added
1 bunch basil leaves, roughly chopped
1 tbsp balsamic vinegar
½ cup water or stock
sea salt and black pepper, to taste

Topping:
2 large sweet potato, peeled and chopped into chunks
parmesan cheese or nutritional yeast flakes (optional)
parsley, to serve (optional)

METHOD

1. Preheat oven to 180°C/360°F.
2. To make the topping, steam the sweet potato until it is cooked through (approx. 7 mins). Mash until smooth and season to taste. Set aside.
2. Heat the olive oil in a large non-stick frying pan over a medium high heat. Sauté the onion, celery and carrot for 3–4 mins.
3. Add the garlic to the pan and sauté for a further 2 mins. Add the mince to the pan and break up any clumps using a wooden spoon. Brown for 3–4 mins, stirring continously.
4. Pour in the rest of the ingredients and bring to the boil. Reduce the heat and simmer for 5 mins.
6. Season to taste. Pour the cottage pie mince mix into the base of a large ovenproof baking dish.
7. Spread the mashed sweet potato over the top and sprinkle with parmesan cheese or nutritional yeast flakes, if using. Bake for 15–20 mins, or until golden on top.

Serving and storing leftovers: Serve immediately topped with fresh parsley, or freeze the completely cold pie on the day you make it, covered tightly, for up to 2 months.

TIP: For a plant-based alternative, swap the mince for an extra tin of lentils.

JESS SEPEL'S ALMOND CHICKEN SCHNITZEL WITH CAULIFLOWER MASH

Nut-free, Wheat-free, Gluten-free.

Prep time: 35 mins Cooking time: 50 mins Serves: 4

This is a healthy take on chicken schnitzel, which is a much-loved classic! I love making this for a chill Friday summer night and it's a great one for kids, they love helping coat the chicken ready for frying.

INGREDIENTS

1 cup almond meal
⅓ cup finely chopped sage, rosemary or thyme leaves
2 free-range or organic eggs, lightly beaten
1 tbsp milk of choice
salt and pepper
2–3 organic chicken breast fillets, sliced in half lengthways or 4–6 chicken tenderloins
1 tbsp olive oil or coconut oil
lemon wedges to serve

Cauliflower mash:
head 1 head cauliflower, chopped into florets
½ cup milk of choice (I use almond milk)
1 tbsp organic coconut oil or organic butter
salt and pepper, to taste

METHOD

1. To make the cauliflower mash, steam the cauliflower over a pot of boiling water until very well cooked, approx. 10–15 mins.
2. Transfer to a food processor and add milk and oil or butter, then process until puréed. If it's too thick, add a little water. Season with salt and pepper. Set aside.
3. In a large shallow bowl, combine the almond meal, herbs and some salt.
4. In a separate large shallow bowl, whisk the egg, milk and season with salt and pepper.
5. Dip the chicken into the egg mixture, then coat evenly in the almond mix.
6. Heat the olive oil in a large non-stick frying pan over a medium heat and cook for 3–4 mins on each side or until the chicken is lightly golden and cooked through. Alternatively, you can bake them in the oven at 160°C/320°F for 35–40 mins.
7. Serve with lemon wedges and cauliflower mash.

Serving and storing leftovers: Serve immediately. Store in the fridge for up to 2 days.

TIP: You can swap any of the animal-based protein options above for 100 g tempeh or tofu (1–2 times a week).

BODY BACK AFTER BABY

WITH SIMONE DE LA RUE, FOUNDER OF BODY BY SIMONE

IT IS IMPORTANT FOR EVERY WOMAN TO FIND TIME TO EXERCISE. IT CAN ACT AS THAT IMPORTANT PERSONAL TIME WHEN YOU GET TO BE ALONE AND FOCUS ON YOURSELF. IF YOU EXERCISE, YOU FEEL BETTER AND HAVE MORE ENERGY, SO YOU WILL IN TURN BE THE BEST VERSION OF YOURSELF, WHICH WILL HELP YOU SHOW UP AS THE BEST MOTHER AND WIFE.

HOW SOON CAN MUMS GET BACK INTO EXERCISE AFTER GIVING BIRTH?

It can be as soon as four to six weeks – and after getting clearance from your doctor – that you can start exercising. I will not see a client before then, as it's vital everything has time to heal and the abdominal wall has time to come back together. Starting too early can cause diastasis recti, and we want to avoid that at all costs.

WHAT IS THE KEY TO GETTING BODY BACK AFTER BABY?

Slow and gradual. It took you nine months to put on the weight, and it will probably take you nine months to take it off. It is important to keep up your calories as you need them for breastfeeding. Actually, cutting your meals while breastfeeding can slow down your metabolism. Work on building your strength and endurance, and be gentle and kind to yourself.

WHAT ARE YOUR EXERCISE DOS AND DON'TS?

Always make sure you understand an exercise correctly, and don't be afraid to ask a trainer in your gym for help. Doing an exercise with incorrect form can cause injury. My number one Do is just to do something every day. Try to do some form of exercise, whether that is just taking the stairs rather than the elevator or walking rather than getting in a cab, even if it's just 10 minutes a day – that's better than nothing.

HOW IMPORTANT IS IT TO MIX THINGS UP WHEN IT COMES TO EXERCISE?

Our bodies and our brains need to constantly be stimulated. Your muscles can get lazy if they are worked in the same way each day. You need to mix it up and continuously shock your system. Mixing it up also helps to keep you inspired and coming back to workouts that you love.

HOW IMPORTANT IS DIET?

It's 80 per cent diet, 20 per cent exercise. I don't like to call it diet, instead I refer to it as just healthy eating. You must fuel your body for your activity, and make healthy choices. You're not going to see results and the desired benefits if you exercise and then eat a pizza. I'm all about balance, and fueling your body with healthy food that helps you thrive is the best default.

SIMONE DE LA RUE

CELEBRITY PERSONAL TRAINER,
FOUNDER OF BODY BY SIMONE

I created Body By Simone eight years ago, and opened my first studio in NYC before expanding to LA. I wanted a workout that was joyous and left clients feeling invigorated, so my training method combines strength training and dance cardio; it's always new and exciting which is something that I need to keep me loving the workouts.

I wanted to share my knowledge and make my method accessible to everyone around the world. My celebrity following has come about honestly by luck and then word of mouth.

Any time I watch my clients on the big screen for a movie role that we've worked for months on is always such a proud moment. Most recently it was seeing Jennifer Garner starring in *Peppermint*, which we worked so hard towards. Watching Sandra Bullock accept her Oscar, and Taylor Swift win her Grammys, are proud moments for sure. But there are also moments like launching my app and working on *Revenge Body* (with Khloé Kardashian) are both milestones I'm equally proud of.

I have just launched my app, which includes, recommended workout plans from me, live streamed classes from my studio in LA, customised nutrition from Kelly LeVeque, and the ability to create your own customised workouts. I really wanted it to be like having the dream team, nutrition and training, in your pocket for use anywhere, any time.

BODY BY SIMONE

Simone De La Rue has worked with Jennifer Garner, Sandra Bullock, Khloé Kardashian on Revenge Body, *Taylor Swift and Kelly LeVegue to name a few.*

'Be gentle and kind to yourself. It took you nine months to put on the weight, and it will probably take you nine months to take it off.'

CAN YOU GIVE US A TASTE OF A QUICK WORKOUT MUMS CAN DO AT HOME WHILE WATCHING THE KIDS?

This is Mummy and Me Workout from Body By Simone TV which I love. You can actually do it while holding your baby who acts as the weight.
Or alternatively you can have them near you while you complete the circuit with body weight or free weights. With all of these exercises start with as many as you can manage and build up to ten reps. You can also build to two rounds of this circuit. It's important to listen to your body, and go slow and steady to start with.

MUMMY AND ME WORKOUT FROM BODY BY SIMONE

- Back standing lunge, alternating legs x 4 each side
- Build up slowly to 10 reps
- Forward standing lunge, alternating legs x 4 each side
- Build up slowly to 10 reps
- Side lunges, alternating sides x 8
- Curtsey lunge with low side kick x 10 each side
- Bicep curls holding your baby, using both hands to lower and lift your baby in front of you x 10
- Squat with shoulder raise x 10

ADVICE FOR FIRST-TIME MUMS AND PARENTS

HOW YOU CAN ADJUST TO BEING A NEW PARENT

YOU CAN'T PREDICT YOUR LABOUR UNLESS YOU DECIDE ON A C-SECTION

Unfortunately you can never predict how a labour will go or when it will happen, and everyone seems to have a different story from the traumatic to the seamless. Many mums who have elaborate birthing plans of natural, water or home births to name a few, often get extremely frustrated, scared, disappointed and stressed when things don't go to plan, which they most often don't! Even if you do have an elaborate plan that you've been working on for the past nine months, make sure you go into the birth with an open mind. You never know what might happen and the way to cope is to avoid the stress that comes with things not going to plan!

ALL THAT MATTERS IS THE BABY IS BEING FED

If you are breastfeeding, remember it takes time and that's okay. If you plan on bottle feeding, do not let yourself feel like you're doing anything wrong because you decided to do it that way. Many women can't actually breastfeed and have no choice but to go onto the bottle; some babies desperately need formula early on if they are underweight or have difficulties latching on or because mum is simply not producing enough milk. Remember, fed is best!

SLEEP OR REST WHEN YOUR BABY SLEEPS

Remember to take time for yourself when the baby sleeps. Don't start madly cleaning the house and doing all the laundry as you will burn yourself out.

BE PREPARED TO DO A LOAD OF BABY LAUNDRY EVERY DAY

Invest in a large washing machine, because those loads of laundry are going to triple for you. You will underestimate just how many onesies, baby towels, baby clothes and your own clothes you will go through with your newborn.

TRUST YOUR INSTINCTS

Despite how many books you may read or classes you may attend, when bub arrives, trust your gut. You'll be surprised how quickly your mum instincts will kick in. You'll be bombarded with advice from every direction, but only you will know what's best for you and your bub.

MAKE SURE TO TAKE PICTURES

As the years go by and the pictures pop up again, you will be glad you took all those videos and sleeping pics.

YOU'RE GOING TO HAVE SOME BAD DAYS – AND THAT'S OK

Prepare to live in chaos and say goodbye to your well-ordered life! It won't matter if you live in a palace or a wooden hut because you will be too tired to notice and your baby will be crying regardless. These are the days you take them for a walk and listen to the birds sing while you grab your coffee and breakfast on the go.

IT DOESN'T LAST FOREVER

It's true what they say, how quickly time goes when they're babies and that you'll miss the baby stage. During struggles with colic, teething and sleepless nights, you will be wishing it all away until you will want it all back.

DON'T BE ASHAMED OF YOUR BODY

Remember, all new mums have a very altered body after having a baby. You carried for nine months so it will take at least one or two years for your body to normalise again. Don't feel ashamed. Ignore all celebrity postnatal photos. They are not realistic goals to aspire to. Everyone's journey is different. Log off Instagram if you find it's getting you down. Many picture-perfect mums will readily admit those picture-perfect moments on social media took hours and most likely happened right before a baby meltdown.

PRACTISE PATIENCE

There are going to be days when the baby just keeps on crying and the best advice is to place the baby in the crib. Step away. Make yourself a cup of tea and take five minutes.

IT'S OKAY TO ASK FOR HELP

If you think you are suffering from postnatal depression, head to www.panda.org.au – or call their free hotline immediately. If your baby will not sleep, there is no shame in hiring a sleep expert to step in for one or two nights. It will be the best money you've ever spent! For urgent babysitters, try the website www.mothercraft.com.au.

YOU'RE DOING JUST GREAT

You just brought a child into this world and that makes you amazing. No one gets it perfect but you are all doing the best you can and that makes you a superhero!

Photography by Chantel Bianchi

POSTNATAL DEPRESSION

WITH DR FIONA MCGUIGAN, GIDGET FOUNDATION

PERINATAL DEPRESSION AND ANXIETY AFFECTS ALMOST 100,000 EXPECTANT AND NEW PARENTS IN AUSTRALIA EACH YEAR. THIS EQUATES TO 1 IN 5 MOTHERS AND 1 IN 10 FATHERS. THE GIDGET FOUNDATION'S MISSION IS TO RAISE AWARENESS OF PERINATAL ANXIETY AND DEPRESSION, PROVIDING SUPPORT SERVICES FOR NEW FAMILIES STRUGGLING WITH PARENTHOOD.

Pregnancy and the first year of parenthood (the perinatal period) can be a time of great adjustment. Experiencing ups and downs is common to all new and expectant parents, however when bad days start to seriously outnumber the good, women may be at risk of perinatal anxiety and depression. Experiencing the 'baby blues' is extremely common with up to 80 per cent of women experiencing increased emotional reactivity in the two weeks following delivery. However, women who experience perinatal depression will experience higher levels of anxiety or lower mood beyond this initial adjustment period and these symptoms impact their ability to function in their day-to-day life.

PRE AND POSTNATAL DEPRESSION

Perinatal depression occurs when you experience strong emotions impacting negatively on your ability to function in the usual way. If you've experienced low moods that have lasted for two weeks or more, accompanied by a lack of enjoyment or pleasure in life, and an inability to plan for the future, you're most likely suffering from some form of perinatal depression. You're not alone. It affects around 100,000 expectant and new parents in Australia each year. This equates to one in five mothers and one in ten fathers. Men often develop depression and anxiety in the context of a partner's illness – it's understandably difficult to be around a person who is 'down' all the time. Research is increasingly showing that mothers who are experiencing depression find it more difficult to be responsive and sensitive to their infants, with implications for their babies' development and a mother's long-term attachment to their children.

SIGNS AND SYMPTOMS

Signs and symptoms include lower mood and sadness, an inability to participate in activities you used to enjoy before becoming pregnant or the baby's birth, difficulty concentrating, making decisions or getting things done. Physical symptoms include heart palpitations, constant headaches, sweaty hands and loss of appetite, as well as a lack of energy and the feeling of exhaustion. Feeling hopeless or inadequate, pessimistic thoughts, feeling out of control or 'crazy', even hyperactivity have all been reported. Being unable to rest, even when the baby is sleeping is another symptom. Other symptoms include feelings of self-blame and guilt, thoughts of harming yourself or your baby and feeling trapped or in a dark hole with no escape.

Unfortunately many women might not recognise their symptoms as pre or postnatal depression, and may not reach out for help. Women may also fear being labeled as a bad or non-coping mother and be well rehearsed at pushing through and putting on a brave face. Many women do not realise how common the problem is, and that treatment is available and effective.

Dr Fiona McGuigan

GIDGET FOUNDATION

CLINICAL PSYCHOLOGIST

Dr Fiona McGuigan is an experienced Clinical Psychologist and she has experience working in hospital, community and private practice settings. She assess and treats individuals experiencing difficulties with mood, anxiety, trauma, grief and relationship issues. In addition to working in the perinatal field, Fiona also has expertise working with children, adolescents and families with a range of behavioural and emotional concerns.

Gidget was the nickname of a gorgeous, spirited and vibrant young Northern Beaches Sydney mum who tragically took her own life while suffering from unrecognised postnatal depression. As well as a happy marriage and a beautiful nine-month-old baby daughter, Gidget had a wonderful and close-knit family and a really lovely group of friends. Not long after Gidget died, her friends and sisters decided to start the Gidget Foundation in her honour to ensure that what happened to her would not happen to another new mum.

Today the **Gidget Foundation Australia** (gidgetfoundation.org.au) is a really wonderful organisation. It is a not-for-profit that exists to promote emotional wellbeing for expectant and new parents. The Foundation aims to raise awareness of perinatal depression and anxiety (PNDA) among women and their families, health providers and the wider community to ensure that vulnerable people receive timely, appropriate and supportive care. More than 50 per cent of new parents will experience adjustment disorders so the cost to the workplace, the family and the community is significant and poorly recognised. Sadly, suicide remains the leading cause of maternal death.

At Gidget House, a new client will be provided with a confidential, safe and supportive space to talk about their experience and feelings. Medication or referral to a psychiatrist is sometimes also an important component of treatment and a psychologist will work in a close and collaborative manner with any involved professionals.

HOW TO COPE

The most important step for a parent when they are feeling overwhelmed is to talk about their feelings with someone. Sometimes feeling heard and supported by a trusted person is enough to get through an overwhelming time.

For any new parent there are strategies that will help feeling overwhelmed in a particular moment. These include placing your baby in a safe place such as the pram or cot and engaging in a brief breathing or mindfulness exercise, getting yourself and baby out of the house for a walk or coffee and reminding yourself that these strong feelings will pass.

In other instances where the experience of feeling overwhelmed is recurrent and/or accompanied by anxiety or depression, accessing professional help is important. Confiding in a trusted health care professional such as a GP, Early Childhood Nurse, Midwife or Obstetrician is the best place to start. These professionals are able to provide initial support and also determine whether referral to a counselor, psychologist or psychiatrist for specialist treatment and support is a good idea. It is a good idea to access help sooner rather than later or waiting until a crisis point. Research shows that early treatment is associated with recovery and good outcomes for the parent and baby.

ONLINE HELP

IF YOU ARE EXPERIENCING DEPRESSION OR ANXIETY, PLEASE CALL:

PANDA - 1300 726 306 Lifeline - 13 11 14

MOTHERHOOD IS THE GREATEST JOY, THE BIGGEST STRUGGLE, THE INTRODUCTION OF THE JUGGLE, AND WORTH EVERY SINGLE DAMN SECOND OF IT ALL.

STEPH ADAMS & SAMANTHA BRETT,
AUTHORS OF *THE JUGGLE*

THE AUTHORS

Samantha Brett is a news reporter and bestselling author of seven books. Samantha began her journalism career in New York at the Fox News Channel, before returning to Sydney where she was the writer of Australia's number one most widely read column. During that time, Samantha appeared on television stations around the world, wrote multiple books and represented numerous high-end brands as well as lent her support to a number of charities.

Samantha turned her focus to news reporting several years ago, filing reports for *Sky News*, *CBS* and *CNN* on breaking local and international news stories. Samantha currently works at the *Seven Network* as a news reporter and presenter. Samantha has written more than 1000 articles for newspapers and magazines around the world on a variety of topics, most recently taking an indepth look at the injustices of the Australian justice system, and the role of female empowerment in society. Samantha is passionate about helping other women to achieve their dreams, and is a proud supporter of a number of charities helping underprivileged women. Samantha is the founder of www.mummasquad.com – a portal helping new mums navigate the difficult early years.

Instagram: @samantha_brett
www.samanthabrett.com
www.mummasquad.com

Photography by Daniel Ho, *One Click Wonders*
Makeup by Samina Malik

Steph Adams is an accomplished name in the publishing world and a leading digital influencer. She is a bestselling author with four published books and editor of *Laqua* magazine.

Steph holds a Bachelor of Arts Degree from Curtin University and has worked as an Art Director for retail giant Net-a-Porter, as well as some of the biggest publishing houses from *British Vogue, Vogue Australia, Donna Hay, Vogue Living, Harpers Bazaar, Elle UK, Marie Claire, Instyle, Grazia, GQ, Belle, Gourmet Traveller, House and Garden* to *Condé Nast Traveler* magazine.

Steph Adams is currently an editor for leading digital and luxury lifestyle magazine *Laqua* magazine.

Supporting charities around the world while empowering women is something very important to Steph.

Having established herself as a successful art director globally, Steph has gone on to collaborate with brands as a creative director, brand consultant, social media and digital strategist, working with premium brands such as Chanel, Waterford Crystal, Estée Lauder, SKII, Cartier, Sheridan, Aerin Lauder, WelleCo and more.

Instagram: @stephadams2012
www.laqua-magazine.com
www.stephadams.com
www.stephadamscreative.com.au

VIKING

UK | USA | Canada | Ireland | Australia
India | New Zealand | South Africa | China

Penguin Books is part of the Penguin Random House group of companies whose addresses can be found at global.penguinrandomhouse.com.

Penguin Random House Australia

First published by Penguin Random House Australia Pty Ltd 2019

Cover design by Steph Adams
Text design by Steph Adams
Cover photography: Natalie Barr by Andrew Finlayson, *The Australian Women's Weekly*, Bauer Media, Australia; Teresa Palmer by photographer Sam Elsom, Creative by Sheree Commerford of Captain And the Gypsy Kid; Louise Roe by photographer Mackenzie Hunkin; Samantha Brett by photographer Chantel Bianchi; Steph Adams by Sugarlight Photography; Elle Halliwell by photographer Bianca Cheah; Megan Gale by Megan Gale; Candice Lake by Candice Lake; Pip Edwards by Pip Edwards.
Printed and bound in China by RR Donnelley Asia Printing Solutions

National Library of Australia Cataloguing-in-Publication data is available.

NATIONAL LIBRARY OF AUSTRALIA

A catalogue record for this book is available from the National Library of Australia

ISBN 978 0 14379 563 6

penguin.com.au